At Home with

Kate

At Home with

Kate

Growing Up in
Katharine Hepburn's
Household

EILEEN CONSIDINE-MEARA

BICENTENNIAL
1807
WILEY
2007
BICENTENNIAL

John Wiley & Sons, Inc.

Published by John Wiley & Sons, Inc., Hoboken, New Jersey
Published simultaneously in Canada

Design and composition by Navta Associates, Inc.

Library of Congress Cataloging-in-Publication Data:

Considine-Meara, Eileen, date.
   At home with Kate : growing up in Katharine Hepburn's household / Eileen Considine-Meara.
      p. cm.
   Includes bibliographical references and index.
   ISBN-13 978-0-471-78376-3
   ISBN-10 0-471-78376-5 (cloth)
   1. Hepburn, Katharine, 1907–2003. 2. Motion picture actors and actresses—United States—Biography. 3. Considine-Meara, Eileen, date. I. Title.
PN2287.H45C66   2007
791.4302'8092—dc22   2006009317

Printed in the United States of America

10 9 8 7 6 5 4 3 2 1

For Tom, Jack, Steven, and Grace

CONTENTS

Contents

Illustrations follow page 118

ACKNOWLEDGMENTS

Many thanks to my terrific literary agents, Jane Dystel and Miriam Goderich, for bringing this book to life with their uncommonly good advice, and for their shared vision about the book's direction and value. I was privileged to have Arlen Gargagliano, an extremely elegant wordsmith, work on this project. She taught me how a pro operates from start to finish and never wavered in her commitment to making this book the best it could be. Thanks to Tom Miller, my editor, for sifting through thirty years' worth of memorabilia and tales with masterly edits and expert guidance, and to his assistant, Juliet Grames, for her sharp eye and enthusiasm. To the Hyatt Street ladies, much gratitude for our soup marathon, and Sotheby's, which paved the way for this project. Thanks to my family for their recollections when my memory faltered during the writing of this book. And last but certainly not least, I owe the largest debt of gratitude to my mother, Norah, whose generosity and graciousness know no peer. She engages and entertains solely by virtue of character rather than any belief her stories will stand upon a bookshelf one day.

Prologue

A h, so you're the victim . . . ," Katharine Hepburn pronounced as she scooped me into her warm embrace. She was commanding, yet graceful and strong, and her words made me feel more like a ten-year-old child than a twenty-something bride to be. I pulled back, grasped her hands, and gazed into her smiling eyes. Kate's beauty could knock anyone off his or her feet. I looked at the often-photographed face that I'd known most of my life. There she was, hair pulled back in a loose bun and wearing her characteristic bright red lipstick, dressed in a black turtleneck with a glorious red bell pepper–colored sweater wrapped around her shoulders, beige slacks, and white sneakers. I hugged her to thank her—bridal showers were definitely not Kate's thing and I knew that she had made an exception to come to mine.

Kate maintained a steadfast grip on my upper arm as I led her into a room filled with more than sixty mostly middle-aged housewives, who were noisily sifting through wrapping and boxes, examining a large collection of dishes and kitchen paraphernalia. A hush came over the room as the women noticed who had just joined them. Once again I realized that this

woman, my mother Norah's employer for over thirty years, was a legend. My mother quickly intercepted Kate and gave her a big hug. The fact that Kate had left the sanctity of her New York City brownstone on this chilly Sunday afternoon in 1992 and ventured up to the suburbs was solely due to her devotion to my mother, a woman with whom she'd shared decades of her life.

Katharine Hepburn was a part of my life from the time I was a little girl. Kate was a role model whose virtues were constantly extolled in my home. From the beginning of my mother's employment with Kate, my siblings and I were drawn into the fabulous whirlwind of Katharine Hepburn's existence. This book is a tender recollection of this American icon. Including photos, recipes, notes, personal letters, drawings, and other mementos, *At Home with Kate* is peppered with anecdotes about the star's celebrity friends, as well as slice-of-life stories that reflect her daily routine. This book is sparked by Kate's quick wit and intriguing character; it presents a personal perspective never before seen by those outside the small circle of Kate's family, friends, and employees.

In 1972, when I was nine, my mother, Norah (originally named Noreen, but called mostly Norah by Kate and her circle of friends) Considine, was in her thirties and looking for work to help support her five children. She was no stranger to working for wealthy clients; her previous employer had been Abby Mauzé, the only daughter of John D. Rockefeller, who lived in one of the fabulous homes along New York City's Fifth Avenue. Following the encouragement of an agency for domestic help, Norah went on an interview that changed the course of her life. Kate lovingly recounted the tale of Norah's hiring many times during the course of their more than thirty-year relationship. "She was the only applicant who stood up when I entered the room. Now tell me, how could I let her go?"

Kate soon became an important part of all of our lives. Mom often enlisted my sister's and my help at the Hepburn residence; my brothers were also called upon on occasion. The way Mom saw it, we could all benefit not only from developing a strong work ethic but also from learning from one of the strongest, smartest, and most talented women she knew. Rather like an aunt, Kate never stopped offering assistance, support, and advice; she sought to make sure that everything was okay in our lives. When my godfather, Uncle Tom, was dying, Kate made sure he was comfortable and well cared for. She went as far as orchestrating a day release from the hospital for a last visit with his family in his own home. When my father was sick, Kate was a frequent visitor and a great advocate for him until he passed away. We all came to depend on Kate in all kinds of situations. When I was dating someone my mom didn't approve of, it was Kate who intervened on Norah's behalf (and yes, I did break up with him after that). Two of my brothers—both die-hard Yankees fans—reaped the benefits of Kate's connections and were able to add (among other things) two signed baseballs to their memorabilia. My brother Pat, who is incredibly handy, was usually called on to help with the painting of the town house at 244 East Forty-ninth Street. He would have loved to have done more, but Kate was reluctant to change anything in her house! My brother Joe had a very special relationship with Kate; like Mom, he carried a lot of worries on his shoulders, especially after my father died. When Mom told Kate that Joe worried about Mom's late nights at 244, Kate told Mom she was lucky to have such a concerned son. When Billy, my youngest brother, had his heart set on attending Boston College and Mom expressed concern about his being accepted there, Kate wrote a letter to the school's president. And in our day-to-day lives, Kate was constantly sharing her words of wisdom, which we usually took to heart.

The living room at Fenwick, Kate's Connecticut mansion.

Norah and Kate arranging flowers in Kate's New York living room.

Of course, Kate also came to depend on us. Whenever she needed Mom to be with her outside of Mom's usual hours, Mom would be there, often with my sister and me in tow. On occasion, Kate could be quite demanding. But she and Mom had a very special relationship, in which the roles of employer and employee were blurred with those of close friends. They were always honest and respectful with each other—maybe that's what kept them so close for so long. As Kate grew older and her health started to decline, Mom cared for her and made sure she was comfortable. From the start of their relationship until its end, their mutual love and admiration was obvious to all.

During the course of Mom's time with Kate, Norah not only met and served an incredible cast of characters—from Sidney Poitier to Warren

Beatty—she also learned what it meant to live as an American icon who was sought out, stalked, and constantly solicited. Mom said she never envied her boss; she saw that there was a very high price for being so famous. It's because of this that despite my mother's great love of theater, film, and music, she steered the five of us away from careers in those areas.

Though my time with Kate was not nearly as extensive as that of my mom, I did spend weeks at a time at the Hepburn New York City and Connecticut residences and was often called on to help out at dinner parties and intimate celebrity gatherings. In addition, Kate frequently appeared at and contributed to landmark events in our family's life. She spent time with us during periods of great sadness as well as joy. Not long ago, I realized that my experiences were unique; when I told my friends some of the tales of life at home with Kate, they oohed and aahed and suggested I write them down. This idea became a plan when after Kate's death, my mom shared a treasure chest of memorabilia—photographs, letters, invitations, and postcards—that Kate had bestowed over the course of thirty years. I share the best of them with you in this book.

The Mayor of
Forty-ninth Street

I t's hard to say who took care of Kate before Mom arrived. Kate would certainly have a laugh at that because she always thought that *she* was in charge of everything! But Mom says it was a toss-up between Charles, hired in 1932 by Kate's then husband, "Luddy" Ogden Smith, and Phyllis, Kate's secretary, hired in 1955.

At the time he hired Charles, Luddy was concerned about his wife's safety; he wanted someone to drive her around and be on hand to protect her, whether at home or out at a show, from the fans who often approached her in New York City. Charles fit the bill perfectly. The former amateur boxer, who was a streetwise character, actually didn't drive Kate around too much; she was adamant about doing the driving herself. But Charles was great at taking care of his boss and the things she needed done around the house and garden.

Kate's garden was one of her prized possessions. She took great care in maintaining the gardens both at her estate in Fenwick, Connecticut, and at 244 East Forty-ninth Street, a four-story town house built in the 1860s in the Turtle Bay neighborhood of New York City. When she wasn't in New York, she'd insist that photos of her garden be sent to her. The fall planting

Kate and Charles in the garden at Turtle Bay in the 1940s.

ritual had started long before Norah arrived on the scene and it continued until Kate left Manhattan in 1998. In the early years, Kate, Charles, and Phyllis did the fall planting. If by chance they waited too long and the ground started to freeze, which was frequently the case, they'd ply the ground with pots of water boiled on Kate's six-burner stove. Then each of them, bundled up in a winter coat, would have to take care of his or her own patch: they'd pour the scalding water on top, and, spades in hand, unearth the stone-cold ground to get the bulbs in.

When Norah was hired in 1972, Charles explained to her his boss's vigilant planting routine. He also told her a tale about the time he didn't fulfill his boss's wishes.

In the early 1950s, Kate split her time between California and New York. Charles was in charge of making sure things in New York ran smoothly, and this included taking care of the house and garden, and looking in on guests like Spencer Tracy, who was frequently at 244 even when Kate wasn't there.

Well, one time, when Charles was about to begin the fall planting of tulips and daffodils, Spencer Tracy, Frank Morgan, and the rest of the Irish crew, as Charles called them, were in the dining room with plenty of drinks on hand and a view of the garden. Spencer, the ultimate man's man, called to Charles, who was out in the yard, on his knees, religiously digging the holes for planting, "Come on, Charles! Get in here and join us for a scotch!" Charles got up, brushed himself off, and reluctantly approached the gang around the table. Spencer handed him a glass of whiskey. "That's more like it, right?" he said, giving Charles a slap on the back.

Charles unwillingly took the drink but said he had to return to the garden to finish the job before his boss returned the next day. "Another time," he said as he headed back out the door. "I just want to finish!"

Charles went back outside and resumed digging. Unaware of Spencer's watchful eye, Charles positioned himself so his back was to the windows and slowly poured the whiskey into the cold earth in front of him. He was sure that if he started drinking with that group, he'd never finish the task at hand. Spencer, who was catching it all, called for his buddies' attention. "Will you get a load of that!" Spencer exclaimed as he jumped up. He went to the door and called out again to the gardener. "Come on now, Charles! What the hell are you doing? Are you nuts? Get back in here!"

Charles halfheartedly put down the spade and, in an if-you-can't-beat-'em mode, stepped back inside. Spencer had him pull up a seat beside him, and Charles ended up spending the afternoon—and evening doing his best to keep up with the Irish crew.

Unfortunately, keeping up took a grand toll. The next morning, Kate arrived early to find Charles sleeping in the twin bed she kept in a corner of the kitchen. Charles heard her but was having a tough time shaking off the effects of the previous night's indulgence. His drinking pal, Spencer, was still fast asleep upstairs. Even Charles's embarrassment couldn't get him up in time to hide the evidence, which included dirty ashtrays and glasses and several empty bottles. He shuffled behind Kate as she strode down the hall into the dining room, and stood back as she took it all in. Without saying a word, Kate turned around, briskly walked out to her car, and left for Fenwick. The incident was never discussed between Charles and Kate, but Mom knew that Charles always felt a bit guilty about disappointing his beloved boss.

I grew up in a totally urban area of the Bronx, and discovering Kate's garden at 244 East Forty-ninth was a thrill; there were paths, trees, and lots of flowers. Just after Mom started working for Kate, I was playing around with a broom that my mom had handed me as she asked me to sweep the leaves from the path that led to the shared gardens beyond Kate's garden gate.

That's when I first saw Charles. I remember looking up at his thick white hair—he looked grandfatherly yet sophisticated in his pressed white shirt and slim dark tie. I felt that this person was somehow quite familiar. After Mom introduced us, he asked me if I'd join him for a stroll in the gardens. He spoke with a slight European accent like my mom's; maybe that's why I felt so comfortable with him. Dropping my broom, I let him take me by the hand and lead me to the centerpiece of the gardens: a stone turtle and a fountain. It was magical.

Charles asked me if I liked flowers, and when I said yes, he told me that Ms. Hepburn—the mysterious actress whom I hadn't yet met—loved flowers. He spoke of her with great reverence, boasting of her appreciation of natural beauty.

Charles was liked by everyone in the neighborhood—that's how he earned his nickname: the Mayor of Forty-ninth Street. Kate appreciated Charles's ability to maneuver everything from leaky faucets to jam-jar lids

Charles and me in the garden of
Kate's house in 1972.

that wouldn't budge, as well as his fine driving and navigational skills during those rare occasions when she wasn't driving or had lost her way. What
Kate most appreciated was the security of knowing that she could depend
on him to handle a wide range of situations. Charles gave Kate the feeling
that everything was going to be just fine.

Something Kate could not count on Charles to handle for her were visits from the billionaire Howard Hughes. Charles disliked Hughes, and
whenever Charles heard the famous producer coming in one door of Kate's
house, Charles would make a beeline out another. Kate would have to
come and attend to her visitor herself.

During Charles's forty-three years with Kate, he earned fame as the
local leader of the pack. Whenever the actress was away filming, he would
gather all of his neighborhood friends: cooks, doormen, chauffeurs, and

any other locals who worked nearby. They would meet in Kate's kitchen, begin with a conversation, and inevitably finish with a grand old Irish sing-along, shoulder to shoulder, beers in hand, and bittersweet tears brimming in everyone's eyes.

When I was a young teen, Charles's health prevented him from working, and he retreated to the house that Kate had bought for him in New Jersey. One day when Kate was away shooting a film in California, my mom, who missed Charles terribly, took a bus out to visit him. During that visit, which unfortunately was the last time my mom would get to see him, Charles walked Norah around his home. He showed her—with the same veneration with which he had shown me Ms. Hepburn's flowers years earlier—his collection of snapshots from all the movies his beloved employer had made.

Cooking Lessons

Though it's hard to believe, Norah really wasn't much of a cook before she worked for Kate. Sure, she *could* cook—she was cooking for five kids and a husband. But her dinner menus were basic: meat and potatoes. So upon her employment in 1972, she was pressed with the need to expand her repertoire—especially since Kate was particular about having fresh soup and vegetables every day. She was also insistent that any leftovers be reinvented into new dishes. Luckily for Mom, Kate liked simple cooking—for example, prime rib prepared with just a sprinkle of salt and pepper. Mom still talks about her first days in the Hepburn household as a time when she was terribly nervous about what she served. "When comments were favorable," Norah tells us, "I would thank God for being on my side!"

Because of her insecurity in the kitchen, Mom welcomed Phyllis's initial gift of a three-ring binder filled with Kate's favorite recipes. Phyllis had been Kate's secretary for nearly twenty years at that point and had carefully documented the foods that her boss enjoyed most.

Another book that Mom found quite helpful was Rus Jones's cookbook. Rus, whose wife was Kate's old friend and financial adviser, was a fabulous

13

cook. One day, when Mom had just started working at 244, her new boss found her thumbing through the leather-bound book of recipes that sat on a shelf in the kitchen next to the binder that Phyllis had compiled.

"Find anything interesting?" Kate asked.

"Well, Ms. Hepburn," Mom remarked as she looked at her boss, "there certainly is a lot here!"

"Let me tell you a story," Kate said as she walked over to Norah and touched the book. "This book here—well, Alice always said her husband was one hell of a cook. Every time they came by, I'd ask him for recipes." She pulled up a chair. "In addition to being a great cook, Rus was very

Kate's kitchen, with the twin bed in the back.

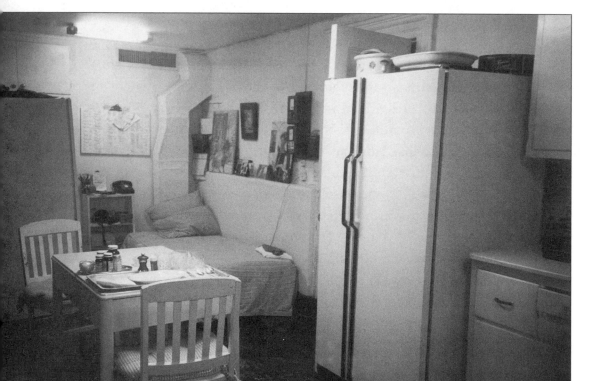

particular about what he ate. I often reminded him that I had asked him to just write down the recipes, and he repeatedly brushed me off with an 'I'm working on it.'" Kate started to chuckle. "But then one day he showed up with this!" Kate smiled broadly as she reminisced. "What a character!" she said.

After that, Mom started experimenting with Rus's cookbook—especially when Kate was away. Before long she had succeeded in expanding her menus, something that her boss was not the only one to benefit from!

Despite what many might think, Katharine Hepburn took most of her meals at home; she never ate in a restaurant during all the years my mother knew her. Kate said that restaurant prices gave her indigestion! When my mother started working for Kate, she quickly learned the rules her boss had regarding food. For example, dinner had to include five vegetables.

Usually Kate would tell my mom, in person or in a note, what she wanted her to prepare. Always frugal, Kate hated to waste anything, especially food. In one particular note, she instructs Norah to prepare soup, a staple in the Hepburn household. My mom developed a repertoire of soups—ranging from beet to lentil, with many in between. Kate also requests that Norah use the vegetables in the icebox (a term left over from her youth) and reminds her that there is leftover mushroom sauce. She then specifies scalloped potatoes, cabbage, zucchini, and squash, as well as cauliflower. The menu ends—as all Kate's meals ended—with a dessert. In this case, it was not one of her favorites—brownies, lace cookies, and ice cream reigned in Kate's dessert world—but apple crumble, one she liked to have on occasion.

Flamande Salad

This Flemish-style salad was popular with Kate—and her guests—in the 1970s. Mom adapted the recipe from Rus's cookbook.

• • •

SERVES 4

4 heads Belgian endive, cored
2 cups cooked and diced potatoes, chilled
1 medium red onion, finely diced
3 tablespoons chopped parsley
½ teaspoon English mustard
5 tablespoons French dressing
1 head romaine, escarole, chicory, or Boston lettuce
   (or a combination of all)

Remove the outer leaves of the endive. Separate and wash the leaves, and cut them into 1-inch pieces. In a large bowl, combine the endive, potatoes, onion, and parsley. Combine the English mustard and the French dressing. Add the dressing to the endive mixture and stir well. Cover and refrigerate for about 1 hour. Serve over crisp romaine, escarole, chicory, or Boston lettuce or a combination.

Generosity

Though many people talk about stars' self-involvement, Katharine Hepburn took an earnest interest in those around her. This was apparent immediately after my mom started working for her. Perhaps she was curious about us because she didn't have kids of her own, and she marveled at the fact that Norah had five of us—besides me, there were Patrick, Maureen, Joseph, and Billy.

After one of her first days working for Kate, Mom returned home and said she had a request from her boss: "Ms. Hepburn wants to see photos of you all." She added, "I don't think she believes I've got five of you!" Confused by such a remark, none of us minded that Mom brought over photos for her boss to see. But we were a bit surprised by the results.

The first thing that Ms. Hepburn noticed in the photos was the fact that my sister, Maureen, had a mole under her right eye. Without delay, Kate had Mom take her to a dermatologist to have it removed.

Next, Kate studied my picture. "Oh, dear," commented Ms. Hepburn. "Her teeth—they're not very good, are they?"

Well, they weren't. But at the time, Mom didn't have the extra money to take me to an orthodontist. Though Dad worked two jobs, as a bartender

My siblings and me. Clockwise from top left:
Maureen, Patrick, me, Joseph, and Billy.

during the day and as a subway clerk at night, and Mom worked hard at this new one, they were struggling just to get by. Mom held back a response, not wanting to reveal her economic situation to her new boss.

But Kate didn't forget about my teeth. By the end of that week, Kate had spoken with her Central Park West dentist and requested that he take me on as a patient.

As it turned out, I needed the works: extractions, a root canal, and, of course, braces. The whole ordeal took about three years. Kate footed the entire bill, never once asking me or Mom questions that would have made Mom feel guilty about her incredibly generous gift of good teeth.

Afterward, Kate always told me I had a beautiful smile.

In my communion dress before my teeth were fixed.

Drawing

Katharine Hepburn brought her gifts for artistic expression to most of the world via the movie screen and her books. What few know is that Kate also loved to draw.

Many times during the course of Norah's duties either at the New York City brownstone or up in Connecticut at Fenwick, Mom would come upon her boss drawing pictures. Ms. Hepburn primarily enjoyed doing self portraits. Her rough-lined illustrations, though done simply, conveyed a great deal of emotion—like the grande dame herself.

One day in New York, Mom went to look for Kate after not having seen her for several hours. Still holding a kitchen towel, she climbed the stairs to Kate's living room and found her sitting in front of the hearth, one of her favorite spots, enjoying a blazing fire—in the heat of summer, mind you—and happily focusing on her pen and sketch pad.

"Hello, Norah," Kate said, eyes still glued to her illustration.

"Why, Ms. Hepburn, I was wondering what you were up to!" Mom exclaimed. She was about to head back downstairs and give her boss the private time she desired, but something held her back. She looked over at

Kate, who now held up her artwork for inspection. Mom saw that it was one of her many self-portraits, and she stepped closer to examine it.

"Do you want it?" Kate asked, somewhat critical of her work but apparently inspired by Norah's interest.

"Oh yes," Mom replied. "It's lovely, Ms. Hepburn."

"Great!" responded Kate. And with a flourish, she tore the sketch from the pad and handed it to Norah, who received it with genuine pleasure and appreciation. She looked back at Kate to continue the conversation, but her boss was already moving on to the next sketch . . . pen in hand, eyes focused on the paper, face glowing in front of the fire she loved so much.

Irene Selznick

Kate's generosity came in many forms; one of them was that she often shared my mom with her friends. One afternoon in 1974, while Kate was away working on a film, she called Norah. "Irene needs a hand," she began. "Be a dear and go over to the Pierre to see what she needs." Norah immediately left Kate's brownstone and headed toward Fifth Avenue to the Pierre Hotel, where Irene lived year round.

Irene was Irene Selznick, the daughter of Louis B. Mayer of Metro-Goldwyn-Mayer, one of Hollywood's most powerful tycoons. A friend of Kate's up until her death, Irene, a successful, wealthy theater producer, came for dinner often.

Like her friend Kate, Irene was not shy about giving advice. My mother learned that very early on. One day, while Mom was helping Irene in her home, they started talking about Norah's employer. Irene, already familiar with Mom's personal history, including her being saddled with the five of us kids, said, "Well, Norah, you may not have an education, but being around Kate will be a great experience for you. It will open doors for you *and* your children."

Norah likes to tell one particular story about Ms. Selznick's observations. Norah had received, in packages carefully bundled from Ireland, glasses made of Waterford crystal. The present had come from the Griffeys, the family that practically raised Mom. Not wanting to keep the special gifts at home, where they had a great chance of becoming splintered shards, she brought the elegant glassware to Kate's for safekeeping. One evening during the early 1970s, Mom decided that she would dispense with Kate's usual place settings (which were quite simple—even paper at times!) and use her own elegant Irish linen and Waterford glasses. As the guests filed in for dinner, Irene gently pulled Mom aside. "Norah dear," she whispered, "this looks so gorgeous, and I know it's all your doing! Nice work." She gave Mom's arm a light squeeze. Mom grinned with pride and lightly touched Irene's hand before she headed back to the kitchen. "Thank you, Ms. Selznick," she said.

Chicken Loaf

(Adapted from Irene Selznick's recipe)

• • •

3 cups finely diced yellow onions

2½ cups finely diced celery

3 cups diced carrots

½ package (9 ounces) frozen French cut string beans,
    cooked and diced

1 teaspoon chopped parsley

3 eggs

2½ pounds ground chicken

3 slices white bread, crusts removed

2 cups chicken broth

Black and white pepper to taste

Salt to taste

Thyme to taste

Marjoram to taste

Additional herbs as desired

Preheat the oven to 350° F. Pour about ½ cup water into a Dutch oven on top of the stove and bring to a boil. Steam the onions, celery, and carrots individually. When you've removed the last batch from the pot, drain the water and set the vegetables aside. Add the cooked green beans and parsley.

In a large bowl, beat the eggs. Add the chicken. Place the bread slices in a medium bowl. Pour the chicken broth on top and mash the bread. Add the bread to the chicken mixture. Add the peppers, salt, thyme, and marjoram to the chicken mixture, along with the vegetables, and mix well.

Place the mixture in a buttered, shallow roasting pan, spreading it evenly without mashing it down, and bake for about 1½ hours. Check for doneness. When the loaf is cool, cut it into slices for serving.

A Friend in Need

Katharine Hepburn was a very caring friend and would always try to meet the needs of those close to her.

In the early 1970s, not long after Kate's Tony-nominated performance in *Coco* on Broadway (under Michael Benthall's Tony-nominated direction), Mom received a call from her boss, who was out in California. "Norah, it's desperate!" Kate announced. "I've just gotten a call from London from Michael Benthall. You know who Michael Benthall is, right?" Kate asked.

Norah was busy thinking about who the man was; she was still getting to know the players in Kate's life, and though Kate's close circle was not extensive, Norah had a lot of new names to remember. Not wanting to seem ignorant or rude, she answered, "Of course, Ms. Hepburn."

"Great. Well," Kate continued with a tone of urgency in her voice, "Michael can't get any paper!"

"Paper?" Norah asked, not quite sure she had understood.

"Yes, Norah. *Paper! Toilet paper!*" Kate clarified in an exasperated tone.

"I see, Ms. Hepburn," Norah replied, tickled by the comedy of the situation.

Kate continued, "There's a strike over there. We must help him out!"

Always the dutiful employee, Norah wholeheartedly agreed with her boss. Then she asked, "So how can we help him, Ms. Hepburn?"

Kate had already thought this through. "Go out and get six rolls of toilet paper and airmail them to him today. I don't care *what* it costs—just do it today!"

Mom has the habit of taking on the cares and worries of those around her, so she immediately left to fulfill Kate's wishes. She purchased the

Katharine Houghton Hepburn

III-26-1976

TO WHOM IT MAY CONCERN:

Please be advised that the bearer, MRS. NORA M. CONSIDINE, is authorized by me to transact routine business in my name, including but not limited to picking up and delivery of packages and messages addressed to me.

Very truly yours,

KATHARINE HEPBURN

toilet paper, brought the rolls back to the brownstone, and packaged them for shipping. Then she was off to the post office to complete her mission.

The line at the post office was long, but after about thirty minutes, Norah reached the clerk. She slid the box toward him. "This has to go to London via airmail," she announced anxiously.

The clerk checked the address and kept his eyes lowered as he looked up pricing on a chart. "That's fine, lady, but you need to declare this."

"But why?" asked Norah innocently. "It's just toilet paper."

The clerk looked up at my mom. "Excuse me?" he asked incredulously. "Did you say *toilet paper*?"

Norah launched into an explanation. "Well, sir, in England there's a paper shortage. It's a real problem over there. These are for some friends and they must be sent out today!"

The clerk seemed not to be in the habit of smiling at work, but he looked amused. He filled out her form and stamped the package before looking up at her. He couldn't help a grin as he pronounced, "Well, let's just hope they can hold out till it gets there!"

Norah nodded and left. Once outside the post office, she shook her head and laughed heartily.

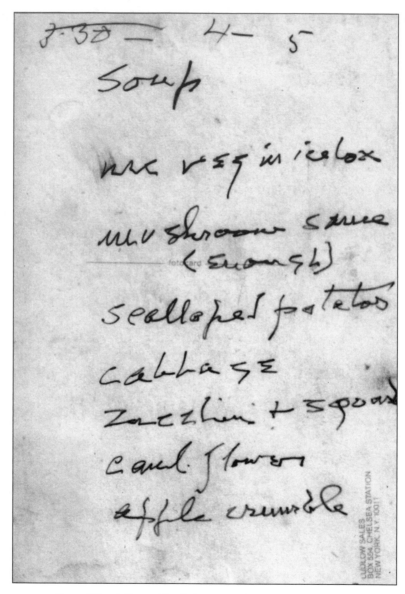

One of Kate's lists of food she wanted Norah to prepare for dinner.

Fenwick

legant and stately, Katharine Hepburn's coastal estate in Old
Saybrook, Connecticut, was magnificent, and she thoroughly
enjoyed her time there. In this serene setting, Kate could stroll
about in town—even take in a movie—without being dis-
turbed. Like New York City, Old Saybrook respected its grande
dame. She loved the freedom, not to mention the gorgeous maritime
advantages of, and views from, her Connecticut residence.

My mother learned early on that she could be summoned to either of
Kate's homes at the drop of a hat—in some cases, at the crash of a wave!

One day in the early 1970s, Kate sent a distress call to Norah. "You've
simply got to get up to Fenwick as soon as possible! Water's coming in on
all sides!" Kate's voice on the phone that day was throatier and more anxious than it usually was. Norah told Kate not to worry and assured Ms.
Hepburn that she'd be there as soon as possible.

My mom was already well versed in the house's history: when Fenwick
was rebuilt in 1938 after a devastating hurricane leveled all parts of the
original house, the builders unfortunately built it too low, so it was below
sea level. (In fact, after Kate died, the new owner quickly rebuilt to rectify

Fenwick.

the problem.) Any flooding in the area would have grave consequences to the estate. Norah made arrangements for a driver to deliver her to Fenwick, and she was imagining all kinds of disasters as they headed up the New England Thruway that day.

When Norah arrived, Kate was alone. She grasped Norah's shoulders with her strong hands and held her momentarily, though to Norah it felt like quite a while. My mom says that Kate's intense gaze had the power to stop time. "Let's get going, Norah. There's so much to do!" Kate pushed Mom in the direction of stacked pails.

Immediately the two women set to work, grabbing pails, filling them with the water and sand that had found its way into the illustrious wooden-floored home, and tossing the slurry outside. They worked hard for hours, side by side. Kate and Norah—equal matches in energy and strength. The water had reached halfway up the sides of the kitchen cabinets. When the women finally got enough water out the door, Norah was horrified to discover the extent of the damage; the floors had buckled from the onslaught. The dining room, with its rear exposure to the Long Island Sound, had suffered the most. Because of the damage, all the wood floors had to be replaced.

Later that evening, Kate's sister Marion and Marion's husband, Ellsworth Grant, came by to check on the exhausted workers. Appreciative of Norah's efforts yet drained by the whole event, Kate mustered the energy to proclaim to her sister and brother-in-law, "No, it's fine now." Kate grinned at the woman who had literally bailed her out and proudly added, "Really, don't worry. Norah and I, well, we've got everything under control."

View of the Long Island Sound from the Fenwick living room.

Kate's Brother Dick

*I*n many ways, Kate's brother, Dick, embodied the idealism that the Hepburn family valued. He also shared his famous sister's spark and persuasive skills.

Dick, Kate's younger brother, and the third of the Hepburn children, lived at the Fenwick home until his death in 2000. He and Kate had a practical living arrangement that allowed them to respect each other's privacy. Kate, well aware of how difficult it was for her kid brother to have his own identity blurred due to her great fame, wanted to live with him in a way that honored his independence. Though they shared the large main kitchen in Fenwick, one side was strictly Dick's and the other was Kate's. The kitchen was ample and held two of everything: stoves, sinks, and refrigerators. According to Mom, Kate and Dick often prepared their meals together, and Dick sometimes cooked for his sister, though he also liked to cook for his family and friends on his own. The arrangement worked out quite well.

Dick was an interesting character. Like his sister, he was in the entertainment field, but he worked a different angle: he was a writer. He penned a number of plays in his lifetime and had some of them produced on the

Dick Hepburn on his side of the Fenwick kitchen.

West Coast and in repertory theaters. Though he never had what one might call a *real* job, he was a talented, Harvard-educated man. He married and had four children.

My mother always enjoyed Dick's company and still can't help but chuckle when she remembers the tidbits of advice he offered her during her time with Kate, advice that ranged from suggestions in food preparation to health tips.

One day many years ago, Mom was up at Fenwick, in the kitchen, preparing one of Kate's favorite lunches: chicken salad with grapes and capers. Kate was quite particular about how she liked this salad prepared—she wanted her grapes peeled. Mom did this without thinking about it; she was always eager to please her boss, so the work didn't bother her. Dick thought the whole grape-peeling thing was silly. He entered the kitchen and shook his head as he watched my mom laboriously take the skin off each grape and cut it in half before adding it to a bowl. She would soon stir the grapes into the chicken salad.

"Norah, my dear," he offered, "here's a trick I use with *that* job." Dick sauntered over to Kate's side of the room as my mom turned from her task, curiously awaiting his suggestion. Taking a grape off the wooden cutting board Mom had been working on, he continued, "I'd say, Norah, it's a much more enjoyable task if . . . you *eat* every other one!" Popping the grape into his mouth, Dick started to walk out of the room—but not before adding, "And don't worry about my sister; she'll never notice! After all, I've been doing it that way for years." With that and a "Good day," he tipped his hat and walked out the door.

Dick also encouraged my mom to do something she had never done

Kate's side of the Fenwick kitchen.

before: swim in the Long Island Sound. Kate, an avid swimmer, barely missed a day—even in winter! Norah, unfortunately, had never learned how to swim, and though she appreciated the beauty of the water that lapped onto the shores of Fenwick and admired her boss's aquatic prowess, she hadn't been able to make herself venture into the sound. But Dick changed that. One day, he questioned my mom as to why she didn't enjoy the refreshing dips that he and his sister were taking. My mom launched into her explanation: "I don't swim, Dick, never have. I don't know what I would do if a wave came towards me and I lost my footing. I'm a bit nervous about the whole wading bit."

Dick responded in characteristic no-nonsense Hepburn fashion, dismissing her fears with a wave of the hand. "Rubbish. Why, it's the heat of summer! Norah, you must get out there and try it!" he commanded.

Norah swimming in the sound.

Kate overheard her brother, and couldn't help but add, "Yes, Norah! Get in there! It's about time—and you'll see, the water's marvelous! Go upstairs. Behind the door you'll find one of my old suits hanging. Borrow it. "

My mother heeded her boss's and her boss's brother's advice. Mom tells the story of dipping into the delicious water in the same awe-filled way a child might talk about eating his or her favorite dessert. Thanks to Dick's and Kate's encouragement, Norah was smitten with the joy of wading in the water. That day, it was very hard for Mom to leave the beach and get dinner started.

Dick Hepburn's Chicken Salad

· · ·

MAKES 4 TO
6 SERVINGS

⅓ cup mayonnaise

1 to 2 tablespoons sweet gherkin juice or the same amount of red wine
vinegar, mixed with 1 tablespoon granulated sugar

3 cups cooked chicken, cut into 1-inch cubes

1 pound green seedless grapes, peeled and halved

1 cup finely diced celery

1 tablespoon chopped capers

1 head Boston lettuce (or ½ head any other kind), torn into small
pieces

In a small bowl, combine the mayonnaise and sweet gherkin juice or vinegar mixture. In a large bowl, combine the chicken, grapes, and celery. Add the capers and the mayonnaise mixture to the chicken and mix well. Spread lettuce leaves onto a serving platter and top with the chicken salad. Serve immediately.

Kate's Candide

*I*n the early 1970s, Kate's director friend Anthony (Tony) Harvey took Kate to a production of *Candide*, the Leonard Bernstein musical with extra lyrics written by Stephen Sondheim. As Kate and Tony entered the theater, they found that their seats were benches. They sat, and Kate turned to Tony and said, "These are the most uncomfortable seats—dreadful. I hope you didn't pay too much money." She was rather grumpy about it.

The play hadn't yet started. Kate and Tony looked down at the stage and saw that the leading actor, who was playing Dr. Pangloss, was lying on a beautiful couch in the middle of the stage. Kate took notice, turned to Tony, and said, "Well, *he* certainly looks comfortable, doesn't he?" Tony said, "Well, I bet you wouldn't go down there and join him." With that, Kate said, "Are you kidding? How much?" Tony replied, "One hundred bucks." "Fine," said Kate, who got up, proceeded toward the stage, and laid down in the center of it with the actor, who looked quite mortified. As the audience realized that it was Katharine Hepburn, they started to laugh and clap. Embarrassed, Kate turned bright red and staggered back to her seat. She said to Tony "My God, what did you do? Now give me the hundred dollars."

From left, Anthony Harvey, Kate, and Peter O'Toole. Harvey
directed Kate and Peter in the film *The Lion in Winter.*

The lights dimmed and the show started. At the end of the show, the
actors gave notes to Kate that said "We love you . . . we love you, Kate."
After leaving the theater, Kate and Tony went back to Kate's town house.
Norah approached with some drinks she had prepared for them.

Suddenly there was a knock at the door, and when Norah opened it
there stood Stephen Sondheim. They could tell by the look on his face that
he was clearly not amused by Kate's antics. Sondheim turned to Kate and
said, "What the hell were you doing up there tonight?" Kate laughed.
Though miffed, Stephen stayed and joined the group for a drink, where-
upon Kate proceeded to tell him the story.

Helping My Family

aybe it was the time she spent caring for Spencer Tracy or maybe it was simply the love she felt for my mother—whatever the reason, Kate was always sympathetic and never hesitated to help my relatives when they became ill. She not only offered advice, she also became an active participant in seeing that they were cared for—from offering assistance to visiting them in the hospital. Her unspoken credo was that if something affected my mom, it affected her.

In 1973, when my godfather, Thomas Considine, was admitted to the hospital at age thirty-one, Mom was devastated. He had been diagnosed with liver cancer just after paying off the last note on a bar he had opened a few years earlier. A hard worker like all my relatives, Uncle Tom had crossed the Atlantic from Ireland as a young boy with just a few quid in his pocket and a head full of dreams. Now, like my dad, Tom had a beautiful wife and five young children. But the news from New York Hospital was not good: the cancer was spreading rapidly.

Kate and her secretary, Phyllis, immediately sprang into action. They started by visiting Tom in the hospital. Kate had him moved to another room so that he would be more comfortable. Then, when there was no hope of his returning home, Kate called my mom with a suggestion.

"Norah," she started in a gentle but authoritative manner, "you know a lot of people. Why don't you find a nurse and we'll get a driver to bring him up to see his family. Let's get him out of that hospital so that he can visit them and he can see his home one last time."

Though Mom was not sure about this mission, she had great faith in Kate, so she went along with the idea. She got her nurse friend Claire O'Dea to accompany them from New York Hospital up to Mahopac, New York. Once Mom got Uncle Tom into the car, she started to greatly doubt Kate's plan—he looked so tired, drawn, and weak. But soon after their arrival, as she took in the scene that unfolded before her, all of her misgivings dissolved.

Uncle Tom arrived home that day to a houseful of relatives. Weak as he was, he was no longer the cancer-ridden patient lying helplessly in a hospital bed but the strong, well-loved, and accomplished family man returning home. As he exited the car, he had a sudden spring in his step; he sparked up to greet his wife, children, nieces and nephews, and brothers and sisters. Our hearts swelled with the realization that his visit home was a rare and precious gift. With tears in our eyes, we took turns embracing Uncle Tom.

Thomas Considine passed away shortly after that day. Mom and I often talk about Uncle Tom's zest for life. And of course, we can't help but talk about the gift dear Kate gave us.

Kate's Only Husband

Though Kate's marriage—to socialite businessman Ludlow "Luddy" Ogden Smith—lasted only six years, Luddy maintained his close ties to Kate until his death in 1979. Always a gentleman, Luddy's high esteem and deep love for Kate were obvious to Norah.

Whenever Luddy traveled to New York on business (from his home in Connecticut), he would stop by Kate's on Forty-ninth Street. One time, as Kate and Phyllis were heading out, Luddy made one of his unexpected visits. Kate had an important engagement, and she had to leave. Grabbing her coat and bag, with Phyllis in tow, Kate greeted Luddy and apologized for having to run. As she practically knocked him over in her haste, she assured him, "Norah will take care of you." Hand on the doorknob, she shouted across the room to Mom, "Norah, feed him!"

Luddy settled into the dining room and read the paper as my mom prepared one of her impromptu fabulous lunches. This day she served creamed chipped beef on toast to the sole diner. They conversed easily about one of their favorite topics: Ms. Hepburn. Though Norah was always discreet when it came to talking about Kate, she did share some amusing anecdotes about recent guests and adventures. Luddy also asked about my mom's health and about her family. He listened attentively, as always, and finished up his dessert of coffee and homemade cookies.

As Luddy was thanking Mom and preparing to leave, he handed her a piece of his personalized stationery. The fact that it was printed with "Ogden Ludlow" tickled Mom, who knew that Kate had requested that Luddy change his name from Ludlow Ogden Smith to S. Ogden Ludlow; Kate didn't want to be known as Mrs. Katharine Smith because it was too ordinary. Above his name, Luddy had typed a title: Shrimp Lime Ring—serves 4. This was followed by the date, a list of ingredients, and the thirteen steps that were required to prepare the dish. Luddy smiled at Mom as she studied the recipe. "Norah, you simply must make this for Kate! She'll love it."

As she said good-bye, my mom assured him that she would prepare the dish, but she knew how her boss would react—recipes that appeared the slightest bit involved were not Kate's style. Sure enough, when Kate returned home and Norah shared Luddy's recipe, Kate glanced at it and said, "Oh, Norah, forget it." She handed it back to my mom and, as Norah had predicted, concluded with, "This is far too complicated!" Norah was careful to later reassure Luddy that Kate had loved the dish.

There were times when Mom didn't travel to Fenwick with Kate. Luddy's was one of Kate's favorite pit stops when she traveled from Fenwick to New York. On those days Luddy would give Norah the cue to start preparing for Kate's arrival in New York in the form of a phone call and a warning: "Okay, Norah, get ready. You've only got forty minutes!" Dear Luddy never knew that Kate was onto him.

Kate was very particular about everything from how pots sat on the stove to how her wooden hairbrushes were washed. Knowing Kate's likes and dislikes, Norah never made the mistake she had made once: not having brownies or lace cookies ready upon Kate's return to New York City. That day, being the woman she was, Kate installed herself in the kitchen and started making the treats she desired. As she mixed the batter, she

SHRIMP LIME RING – serves 4   6/11/76

OGDEN LUDLOW

174 GREENLEY ROAD · NEW CANAAN, CONN. 06840

2 lbs green shrimp
1½ cups pink grapefruit meat (2-3 grapefruit) Don't core. Slice
   both sides of membranes and lift out meat. *START FROM OUTSIDE IN*
1 pkg lime jello
½ cup chopped celery (2 large stalks)
½ cup half mayonnaise/half sour cream, 1 tsp lemon juice, little salt
2 cups same for sauce- 2 tsp lemon juice- little salt
few sprigs of watercress

----

1. in large pan make courtbouillon of 2cups water, 1 cup dry vermouth,
   salt, celery, onion, bayleaf, parsley, tarragon, peppercorns. Simmer
   20 minutes.
2. Add shrimps, bring to boil, cover, turn off flame and let sit until
   cool. *(5MIN) POUR OFF WATER + FILL WITH COLD*
3. Drain and cool shrimp in cold water in same pan (after throwing out
   herbs) and put in refrigerator.
4. Mix gelatin as per directions: 1 cup boiling water, stir, and add 1
   cup cold water.
5. With beater beat in ½ cup mayonnaise/sour cream until thoroughly
   blended.
6. Add and stir grapefruit meat and celery, spreading evenly.
7. Wipe a 10" mold (Kraemer70 or similar) lightly with corn oil, and
   pour gelatin mixture into it. Cover with oiled paper, place in refrigerator for several hours, preferably over night.
8. When ready to serve, devein shrimp and wash in cold water.
9. Place mold in warm water for 15 seconds in sink, cover with silver
   dish and quickly invert. Gelatin ring should drop cleanly onto dish.
10. Pour sauce into silver bowl and serve when ready.
11. Serve with heated dinner rolls.
12. Pile shrimp into center of ring and garnish with watercress.
13. To make half the recipe (for 2) use 7½" ring (Kraemer 50)

teased Norah, "So what have you been doing while I was away?" Of course Kate knew that Mom had been incredibly busy during that time: the phone never stopped ringing, there were deliveries of flowers and the mail had to be sorted and arranged (Mom helped Phyllis out with the mail), and there was always shopping to be done. The last thing Norah wanted was to have Kate in the kitchen.

Mom was always grateful for Luddy's calls.

Mass for Spencer

Norah's routine at 244 East Forty-ninth Street was generally consistent. Typically she would arrive at about ten in the morning and immediately go down to the basement to change from street clothes into a black uniform with a white apron. Then she'd go up to greet her boss, who was always ready to deliver instructions for the day. Kate loved the fact that Mom could listen to a litany of things to do and take mental notes. Kate was also impressed with the fact that from shopping lists to phone numbers, Norah could commit everything to memory. In fact, whenever Kate needed a number, she used Mom as her phone book!

Because Kate usually gave spoken directions, Norah was taken aback when one day in 1974, Kate left very specific written instructions. Ms. Hepburn was setting up a service to honor the memory of her true love: Spencer Tracy, who had died in June 1967.

Kate was not Catholic—in fact, she was once quoted as saying she was an atheist—but she was spiritual, and she was very respectful of Spencer's—as well as my mom's—devotion to the Catholic Church. Perhaps there was a part of Kate that felt Catholic; whenever Mom went off to

Spencer Tracy.

visit Saint Patrick's Cathedral, on Fifth Avenue, her boss would ask her to say a little prayer for her.

The day that Norah arrived to find the lists for Spencer's mass, she learned about all the provisions her boss had made. Apparently Kate had arranged to have Spencer's priest, Father Eugene Kennedy, fly in from California to perform a service in her brownstone.

Father Kennedy arrived before Kate the day of the mass, so Mom got a chance to chat with him privately. He was as eloquent as Kate had described, as well as handsome and warm. (He stayed friends with Kate and visited her regularly until she passed away thirty years later.) When Kate and Phyllis arrived home that day, Norah excused herself to make lunch. "No, Norah dear," began Kate as she reached out for Mom's hand. "Just leave it." She pulled Mom back into the living room and announced, "Okay, Father. We'll start the mass now."

Mom had imagined things quite differently—she had even set up a kind of altar where she thought Father Kennedy could stand to deliver his sermon. But he preferred a much more casual approach. He sat on the edge of the white cotton couch, leaning in toward Kate as she sat back in her favorite chair. Phyllis and Mom were in chairs nearby.

Father Kennedy's mass was a personal and touching tribute to Spencer. He talked about Spencer's life, highlighting his achievements. Ms. Hepburn

Kate and Spencer in the 1945 film *Without Love*.

glowed with a pride tinged with sadness. Mom, having lost her brother-in-law not long before, sympathized with her boss's heartache. She was honored to be included in this very private service. Once it was over, and the ladies had had Communion, Kate thanked Father Kennedy, and they went downstairs to enjoy lunch together.

A casual shot of Kate and Spencer on the set in the 1940s.

Visiting Aunt Jenny

Part of Kate's charm was her girlish sense of humor. She was graceful and sophisticated, but the thrill of a joke, a pun, or a silly misunderstanding could send Kate into hysterics not unlike those of a fourteen-year-old at a slumber party. And though Kate shied away from being the center of attention in many public settings, at home she was the queen. Kate's dinner parties gave her an opportunity to recount her amusing adventures.

One evening in the mid-1970s, my mother was serving dinner to Kate and several guests. As they finished up the main course, Kate began her story.

"Listen," she said as she delicately placed her fork and knife together on the plate to indicate the meal had ended, "I have the funniest story to tell you." Kate's eyes twinkled. "Really—it's just priceless."

The guests, following their hostess's example, placed their silverware down and begged her to continue as my mom entered to clear the plates.

"Well," Kate started in her breathy voice, "before I began shooting *Love Among the Ruins* in London last year, my dear housekeeper, Norah," she continued, smiling impishly at my mom, "pulled me aside with a request.

'Please, Ms. Hepburn,'" she said in her best interpretation of my mom's distinctive Irish accent, "'if you could, stop by and say hello to my aunt Jenny. She's an old woman now living in a retirement home outside Brighton. She was very good to me, and she's got no family left. It's been so long since I've seen her, and I just would like to know if she needs anything.'"

The guests smiled politely and looked quizzically at Mom, then back at Kate, who, delighting in the intrigue, kept speaking.

Kate in Ireland.

"Oh, that's so typical of Norah." Kate reached over to gently touch my mom's arm as Norah cleared the last of the dinner plates. "She always thinks of others before herself."

"So," Kate resumed, "Phyllis and I decided to comply with Norah's wishes and, on a day I wasn't needed on the set, we went to pay the aunt a visit. You have to remember that we were energetic but not quite spring chickens. Just imagine how we looked traipsing across the great lawn to approach the front entrance of the stately brick retirement home where Norah's aunt Jenny was residing!" Kate glanced over at Phyllis, who'd not only lived the story but heard it told many times before, yet always listened attentively as though she was hearing it for the first time.

Kate continued, "There we were, just the two of us, standing at the door. I was wearing my usual outfit—black turtleneck, red sweater around my shoulders, beige slacks, and white Keds— and Phyllis wore her usual button-down blouse, skirt, and *orthopedic* shoes." Chuckling, she went on. "So we ring the buzzer and ask for Aunt Jenny. Suddenly this very proper creature comes to the door, identifies herself as Jenny Kelly, looks us over, and asks what she can do for us.

"I step back a bit and clear my throat as I introduce myself—but I can see she hasn't got a clue as to who I am and on top of that she's fixated on my old duds. So I go on, 'Actually, your niece Norah asked me to come; she works for me in America and thought that if you needed anything, perhaps I could help you.'" Kate's giggles vibrated in her chest. "So Aunt Jenny looks at me, and in her prim and proper manner, exclaims incredulously, '*You?* She works for *you?*' I can still see her: arms folded, wearing a perfectly starched nurse's cap, staring down at my sneakers and moving up slowly to my bun."

Dabbing the tears of laughter from her eyes with her napkin, Kate looked toward Phyllis, who nodded her on. The guests were right where she wanted them: anxiously awaiting the punch line.

The storyteller cleared her throat and sipped a bit of water before trying to get the next couple of lines out. "So then . . . then Aunt Jenny says to me, shaking her head in disapproval, 'Well, if she's working for *you*, she must be in bad shape!'"

From the kitchen, my mom could hear Kate's guests burst into laughter.

"Isn't that the best? Here Norah was so worried about her aunt, and Aunt Jenny was doing better than any of us!" Kate concluded as she lightly slapped the table.

In the kitchen, putting the final touch on the platter of cookies she was about to present, Norah knew Kate was using her napkin once again to wipe away the happy tears.

Jack Larson

Creamed chipped beef, the wonderful comfort food that's said to be a U.S. military breakfast staple, was also a favorite with one particular guest at 244: Jack Larson, who played Jimmy Olsen on the TV series *Superman*. Mom served Jack his preferred lunch treat on several occasions.

Apparently Kate became friendly with Jack while she was filming *Suddenly Last Summer* with Montgomery Clift in 1959. Jack Larson came to visit and care for his friend Monty, who had taken ill; through Monty, Jack met Kate. After the film, Jack stayed in touch with his new friend. He visited her on numerous occasions in California, bringing her treats of dark chocolate turtles, one of her favorites, and taking her out for Brown's hot fudge sundaes. Later Kate would say that those Los Angeles goodies were severely missed in New York!

One day while Kate and Jack were having tea, Jack announced his plans to go see *Equus*, the hit London show that was playing on Broadway with Anthony Hopkins, whom Kate had worked with in 1968 on *The Lion in Winter*. In her characteristic bordering-on-demanding way, Kate requested that Jack get her tickets as well. "You get me two tickets, because I want to go!" So Kate, after promising dinner and transportation to Jack, brought her secretary, Phyllis, along, and they all went to the theater.

According to Norah, who laughs every time she tells this story, what happened after the play was what greatly surprised Kate. Ms. Hepburn was seated in an aisle seat next to Jack; Phyllis was on Jack's other side. Once the curtain came down, a crowd of people came up, clamoring for Jack's autograph (Kate was famous for not giving out her autograph). Bypassing the superstar on the aisle, the fans reached around her. Kate leaned back and said to Phyllis, but not out of earshot of their host, "What *is* Jack doing? Is he signing *my* name?"

Meanwhile, Jack was delighted to fulfill the fans' requests, and his willingness to do so and the fact that he was, in fact, highly solicited were surprising to Kate, who, as I suspect, may have felt a tinge of jealousy. Quickly tiring of the surrounding crowd adoring her friend, she called to Phyllis, went backstage, and graciously congratulated the performers, though according to Mom, she thoroughly disliked the play!

Norah's Creamed Chipped Beef
on Toast

• • •

SERVES 2 TO 4   ½ pound dried, sliced beef
2 tablespoons salted butter
2 tablespoons all-purpose flour
1 cup evaporated milk
Pinch of sage
Salt and pepper to taste
4 slices toasted wheat bread

Separate the slices of dried beef and soak them in hot water for 10 minutes to remove some of the salt. Drain. In a skillet, melt the butter over medium heat. Blend in the flour, and using a wooden spoon, stir it into the butter. Gradually, still stirring, blend in the evaporated milk. Season with the sage, salt, and pepper. When all the ingredients are mixed, add the drained beef to the cream sauce. Lightly butter the slices of hot toasted bread and then spoon the beef over them.

Fans

Kate had many, many fans. Her fans included those who sent her short, sweet postcards and those who asked for favors and money. One group sent her packages of goodies, ranging from chocolates to bedding. Like many stars then and now, Kate was not fond of having her privacy invaded. However, unlike many of her peers, she took the time to personally read through her mail. And in many cases, she responded.

Mom loved to tell us stories about the fan mail Kate received; some of it really tickled her. "Can you imagine," she'd say, "writing a letter to the great Katharine Hepburn, and getting your letter back with spelling corrections?" She'd laugh herself into a sigh before concluding with "Well, that's Ms. Hepburn for you."

Some of the requests Kate received from fans were for advice. Mom recalls one person who was asking about acting. Kate tersely replied, "I'm not an acting coach." The ones she resented most were those who asked her to send them a signed photograph. She wrote back to one such fan, "It's a big bore—to have to sign sign sign." She added, "I want to know the person on whose wall I hang." Undeterred, fans just kept on writing and requesting.

One of Kate's most ardent admirers was a woman named Alice Hicks. Though Alice never came to 244, she was forever sending letters and packages. She sent money (ten- and twenty-dollar bills) after reading that Kate never carried cash. Norah once discovered a fake twenty-dollar bill with

Publicity photograph.

some kind of advertising on it that another fan had sent to Kate. Mom held up the bill and said, "Oh, look, Ms. Hepburn. Someone sent you twenty dollars. What shall we do with it?"

Without a pause, Ms. Hepburn said, "Bank it!" That was typical of her Yankee frugality.

Other gifts she received from fans included a television set, socks, books, scarves, and on one occasion, red flannel sheets. Kate loved red, but she was horrified by this gift. Mom was hysterical when she told us that story. "Can you imagine Kate sleeping on those bright red sheets?" she asked us. Actually Mom couldn't imagine anyone sleeping on them.

Every time Kate received one of these gifts, she'd shout, "Out, out!" to my mother. Mom simply couldn't bear to throw anything away, so she would busy herself trying to find a home for everything, and she was always successful at it.

One afternoon, Kate had had enough. As she was going through her mail, she came upon the longest letter Alice Hicks had ever sent. After thumbing through it, she saw that the letter—more like a short novel—was no less than eighteen pages long. Kate didn't stop to read it. Instead, she picked up her pen and scrawled a message across the top: "Alice, have mercy on me!"

Helping Irene

I used to think that Mom was the only woman who could capably juggle a family of five and a full-time job. Maybe I'm biased, but looking back, I just don't know how she did it all. With her multitasking skills, she could have been the CEO of a major corporation—but she certainly wouldn't have had as much fun!

Kate was well aware of Mom's talents, so when Irene Selznick called her in a panic, Kate offered Norah's services. Irene's assistant and cook of thirty years had recently retired, and Irene was quite upset. Kate explained to Norah, "I told Irene not to worry. Since I'm going to be in California for the next month, she can have you!"

"Yes, that's fine, Ms. Hepburn," Mom replied. Of course, this wasn't the first time Mom had been sent to work for Louis B. Mayer's daughter, but this time she had a lot going on: Kate had houseguests, Sally and Chet Erskine, who were dear friends of hers, staying upstairs while she was away. With this new assignment, Norah would have to spend the next month going back and forth between Kate's and Irene's homes. But Mom was determined to make it work.

That afternoon, Norah headed over to the Pierre Hotel, where Irene lived year-round, to speak with her. She knew that Ms. Selznick, not unlike her friend Ms. Hepburn, was very particular about things. Mom learned that her job would be limited to cooking and that, initially, at least, she would just be preparing the evening meal. Mom received her first dinner menu from Irene and headed back to 244 to organize herself.

The first call she made was to Louis Armando Vargas, Stephen Sondheim's chef and a good friend of Mom's. Concerned about proving that she was just as adept in Irene's kitchen as she was in Kate's, she was anxious to go over the menu with him. Louis was not only helpful, he was also encouraging, and just going over meal plans with him gave Mom the confidence boost she needed.

Thanks to Louis's daily phone calls, everything was working out well for Mom. Irene was happy, and once the Erskines left Kate's, Ms. Selznick had Mom come to prepare breakfast, lunch, and dinner.

During the course of the month, Mom and Irene got to know each other very well. Before long, Irene started to call on Mom for more than just cooking.

On the evening prior to an outing on producer Sam Spiegel's yacht, Irene asked Mom to help her pack her bags. When that was done, Irene had another job for Mom. Irene confirmed that Mom would be spending the night, since it was late. Then Irene asked, "Norah, will you help me dye my hair?"

Mom had never done that before, but she couldn't say no. "Why, certainly, Ms. Selznick."

"Good," Irene responded, leading her into the bathroom where she had all the necessary tools lined up.

Mom went to work. Approaching the task carefully and methodically, Mom followed Irene's directions and applied the chestnut-brown dye from Irene's roots to ends. The two chatted casually during the process. At the end, Mom was rinsing Irene's hair when Irene sat up with a start. "Norah!"

she yelled as if she had been slapped. "My ear!" Mom gently removed the water that had gone into Irene's ear.

"I'm so sorry, Ms. Selznick," Mom said as she continued rinsing. She couldn't help but think that Irene's reaction was overdramatic. After all, it was just a bit of water in the ear.

And yet, aside from the ear incident, Mom and Irene got on famously. Norah loved to hear the stories that Irene told about growing up in Hollywood, and Irene appreciated Norah's eye and respect for the fine trappings she surrounded herself with. After that month, Irene gave Norah a copy of her autobiography, *A Private View*, which contained many of the tales Ms. Selznick had shared with Mom.

And then it was back to 244 East Forty-ninth Street. "So, Norah dear, tell me about life over at the Pierre," commanded Kate upon her return.

"Well," Mom began enthusiastically as Kate started sifting through the mountain of mail that awaited her perusal, "I loved it! That's some place she has there. Can you imagine, she even let me dye her hair!" Mom waited for Kate's burst of laughter. But Norah was surprised by her boss's response.

"Great," Kate said as she pensively picked up one of the envelopes. "Hmmm. Well, next time, Norah," she added, "you can do mine, too!"

Opening Night Party

The opening of *A Matter of Gravity* on Broadway, in 1976, was a highly anticipated event; the public couldn't wait to see Katharine Hepburn in the theater again and also see the handsome young actor Christopher Reeve, who Kate told everyone was going to be a big star some day. Kate was also happy to be in the New York theater once again. She decided to host a party.

Ms. Hepburn's party at 244 was a big deal. She invited everyone from the principal actors to the ushers, though she did not include the financial backers, producers, and directors. Kate was eager to express her gratitude to all the people who helped make the show a success, proving once again that as quick-tempered and demanding as she could be on occasion, she was always generous and grateful.

I was in high school at the time. Like most high school students, I liked to make some extra cash, and working at Mom's boss's presented me that opportunity. When Mom came home to ask my older sister, Maureen, and me if we'd help with the party, we were happy to do it.

Quite a crowd arrived at the brownstone after that evening's performance! Thanks to the help of her talented sisters Yvonne and Carmel, Norah was armed with dozens of platters of finger food. She had trays with assorted hors d'oeuvres and many more with her famous brownies, lace cookies, and other goodies. Bottles of champagne were kept cooling in the garden.

That evening is a bit of a blur, since we were trying so hard to keep up

A playbill from *A Matter of Gravity*.

with the pace of the party. Kate was great; up in her living room holding court, she was surrounded by her coworkers, who were in awe and somewhat fearful of the incredible star. There we were: one set of sisters dodging masses of people as we distributed tasty treats that were quickly devoured, while the other set worked frantically in the kitchen. Mom was

National Theatre

ROBERT WHITEHEAD   ROGER L. STEVENS
KONRAD MATTHAEI

present

Katharine Hepburn

in

a new comedy

A Matter of Gravity

By Enid Bagnold

with

CHARLOTTE JONES

PAUL HARDING • CHRISTOPHER REEVE • ELIZABETH LAWRENCE

WANDA BIMSON • DANIEL TAMM • ROBERT MOBERLY

Scenery by	Costumes by	Lighting by
BEN EDWARDS	JANE GREENWOOD	THOMAS SKELTON

Directed by

Noel Willman

The taking of photographs and the use of recording equipment are not allowed in this auditorium.

totally focused on her task but as usual kept an eagle eye on all of us. "Watch the glasses," she called to us as she shoved another tray of the savory appetizer we called cheesies into the oven, set out a tray of sandwiches, and artfully arranged a tray of brownies. Mom had her eye on our most pressing need; the glasses were being used almost as quickly as we cleaned them. Mom put Yvonne on dishwashing and drying duty, but Yvonne also had her eye on everything, and she felt she had to get back to helping her sister refill the trays that kept coming back empty. As Yvonne worked tirelessly on glass patrol and we all danced in and out around her, she noticed—through a glance in a well-placed mirror—a handsome, well-dressed gentleman standing calmly near the kitchen door. "Hello, sir, who are you?" she asked, half laughing at his calm in the midst of our craziness.

"I'm the chauffeur, ma'am," the man, Fischer, replied as he smiled back at my aunt.

Yvonne stopped juggling the glasses momentarily and threw him a towel. "Well, come on, then! We have a job for you!" She immediately set Fischer, always a great sport, to work. He didn't miss a beat.

Not unlike Kate's run in *A Matter of Gravity*, the party was a huge success.

Stephen Sondheim's Chef

Many of Mom's relationships at 244 East Forty-ninth Street were built around food, and such was the case with Louis Armando Vargas, Stephen Sondheim's live-in chef. The legendary composer was Kate's neighbor for many years. Though Ms. Hepburn and her talented neighbor never developed a relationship beyond their nods hello, Norah and Louis became quite close. They had much in common: they were both immigrants (Mom from Ireland, Louis from Chile), they both worked for people who were incredibly successful in the theater industry, and they were both total foodies. Louis and Norah shared juicy stories, culinary tools and tricks, tons of food, and of course, recipes. What Louis most requested were Norah's sweets.

Beyond his culinary savvy, Louis was an entertaining man who always had comments and advice to share. Since my mom was cut from similar cloth, their banter was amusing.

"Deary," Louis called to my mom from the doorway at 244 one day. "You didn't forget, did you? Tomorrow night's the cast party for Mr. Sondheim's new show." As his eyes swept the room, he continued, "Norah honey, you promised me a few batches of brownies and at least three tins of those lace cookies, and don't forget the rum cake!"

Louis continued to cast a judgmental eye about the kitchen. "This place always amazes me," he commented, shaking his head. "It's such an old dive! Not even a dishwasher! Tell me, how do you get *anything* done?"

Not skipping a beat, Norah responded, "Oh, don't let it bother you! You're just spoiled, that's all!" She wiped her hands on a kitchen towel and turned to take plates from the cupboard. "Who wouldn't love your kitchen next door?" she asked. "Well, you know Kate couldn't stand a kitchen like that; everything there is too modern for her taste. Now stop your complaining! You're just lucky she's away so I have the time to take care of all *your* demands!"

Louis smiled and headed toward the door, then stopped to confirm my estimated arrival time—I was a struggling student at Manhattan College and never refused the opportunity to help serve at one of Mr. Sondheim's frequent parties. Before Louis left, he offered my mother some additional advice. "Oh, and by the way," he said, with one foot out the door, "make sure that whenever guests come into the kitchen looking for the cook, you do what I do. Correct them. Tell them you are a chef, dear." He turned once again toward the door but not before concluding, "After all, *anybody* can cook." Mom smiled and went back to her sink.

Norah's Rum Cake

· · ·

MAKES 1
CAKE, OR
ABOUT 12
SERVINGS

Butter for greasing the pan
1 package Duncan Hines yellow cake mix
1 package vanilla pudding
½ cup cold water
⅓ cup Wesson or Crisco vegetable oil
3 eggs
½ cup dark Bacardi rum—or better, Captain Morgan's Spiced Rum
1 cup chopped pecans or walnuts

GLAZE
½ stick butter
¼ cup water
1 cup granulated sugar
½ cup 80-proof rum

Preheat the oven to 325° F. Grease a 12-cup Bundt pan, then use about a teaspoon of the cake mix to lightly flour it as well. Using an eggbeater or an electric mixer, combine the cake mix, pudding, cold water, oil, eggs, and rum. Mix until well blended, about 3 minutes. Sprinkle the nuts on the bottom of the pan. Pour the batter on top. Bake for 1 hour, or until a toothpick inserted into the center of the cake comes out clean. Let the cake cool in the pan for 10 minutes, then turn it out onto a wire rack and cool it completely. Using a fork, poke holes throughout the top of the cake.

While the cake is baking, make the glaze. In a medium saucepan, melt the butter. Stir in the water and sugar. Boil for 2 to 5 minutes, stirring constantly. Remove the saucepan from the heat after 5 minutes, then stir in the rum. Combine well, then evenly drizzle the glaze over the cake.

The Irish Mafia

Kate's generosity reached many people in my family. As demanding as the grande dame often was, she never hesitated to give us gifts, along with her precious tales of days past.

It was 1977, and my dad was in the hospital. He was suffering from stomach cancer, and it was hard on all of us. Since my mom couldn't drive, Kate generously offered on more than one occasion to bring her to see him. Maybe it was because she identified with Mom's intense concern for the man she loved or maybe she was trying to boost Norah's spirits. Whatever the reason, Kate never hesitated to give Mom the time and transportation she needed to visit Dad.

My aunt Yvonne joined Mom on one of those visits. The two sisters were almost opposites: Mom was somewhat reserved, while Yvonne, who managed a restaurant, had a come-what-may attitude. Part of that had to do with their age difference—Yvonne was nine years younger than Norah. In addition, my mom had five children, so her priorities were quite different from those of Aunt Yvonne, who had only a husband and a seven-year-old child to worry about. However, like Norah, Aunt Yvonne could hold her own with any of the visitors to 244. Kate appreciated Yvonne's spirit and directness.

On the day that Kate picked up Yvonne and Mom from the hospital, Kate was suddenly reminded of Spencer Tracy. Bubbly Yvonne had just finished telling Kate about her husband, Tom. She was describing one of the first jobs he had, which was sampling liquor for distributors in Ireland, and how much fun he and his friends had had with that particular task! This sparked Kate's thoughts of Spencer, and she began to talk about Spencer and his crowd.

"They called themselves the Irish Mafia." Kate chuckled as she maneuvered her car through Central Park. Kate quickly glanced at Aunt Yvonne, her copilot at the moment. "Oh, but that was before your time!" she added. Yvonne was hungry to hear more. Norah and Phyllis, Kate's long-time secretary and traveling companion, sat in the back, oblivious to the conversation taking place in the front seat.

Kate, spurred by Yvonne's interest, continued. "Phyllis," she called to the backseat, "Spencer and that gang, they were quite a group! What fun it was, right?" Phyllis didn't answer her boss's question. Kate tried to get her secretary's attention, "Yoo-hoo, back there! Stay alive."

Kate repeated her question, and Phyllis replied, "Yes, Ms. Hepburn, they certainly were! It's hard to hear in the backseat, with the wind blowing on us."

Kate rolled her eyes. "Why didn't you say so?" Kate proceeded to roll up the windows so that she could have everyone's full attention before continuing.

"They were such fun! Well, this was way back when in the old days. There was Spence, Pat O'Brien, Frank Morgan, James Cagney, and Frank McHugh." Kate shook her head as she smiled. Mom could catch her twinkling eyes in the mirror. "When those guys got together at Romanoff's in Hollywood, they called it Irish night! And when they were in New York, they would stop by to see me. Great bunch, really . . . so much life," her voice trailed off.

Kate focused on the road. Then, suddenly remembering another tidbit to share, she called back to Phyllis. "Now tell them," she commanded, "about the bed. Go on, Phyllis, tell Norah and her sister why there's a bed in my kitchen!"

Phyllis didn't miss a beat. "Why, Ms. Hepburn," she said in a very serious tone, "I always thought it was for your afternoon naps."

Kate slapped the steering wheel. "*Naps*, did you say? For me or that bunch?" Kate didn't wait for Phyllis to respond before adding, "*Naps*, Phyllis? At four A.M.?" Kate laughed at the thought of those wild times, and the guys who obviously needed a place to put their heads down after a night of carousing.

Upon arriving back at the house that night, Kate was still in the mood to reminisce. While Mom was totally exhausted and not too communicative, Yvonne soaked it all in and asked for more. "Ms. Hepburn," Yvonne began, "Spencer Tracy was a favorite of our father's, being Irish and all. I just

From left, Ernest Hemingway, Mrs. Hemingway, Slim Hayward, Spencer Tracy, George Jessel, and Leland Hayward.

loved him in *The Old Man and the Sea*." Kate, pleased by Norah's sister's genuine enthusiasm, suddenly said, "Hold on, I've got something for you!" as she disappeared from the room.

A few moments later, Kate walked down her stairs staring at the booklike square in front of her. Then she handed Aunt Yvonne a precious and heartfelt gift: a photo of Spencer Tracy and his pals. "I've jotted down their names on the back—so just turn it over if you want to know who everyone is.

"Quite a bunch." Kate smiled and crossed her arms, enjoying Aunt Yvonne's gratitude.

Katharine Houghton

Most people remember Kate's niece Kathy as the dazzling redhead in the role of the young woman who brought Sidney Poitier home to meet her parents, played by Katharine Hepburn and Spencer Tracy, in *Guess Who's Coming to Dinner*. Many say that the twenty-one-year-old actress evoked memories of her aunt at that same age. To my family, Kathy has been—and remains—a dear and close friend.

As a niece, Kathy was consistently attentive and loyal; she looked on her aunt as a role model and held her in the highest regard. And Kate thought the world of her intelligent and talented niece. Kate often spoke about Kathy to Norah. She would say, "Kathy's much too smart for this business." Kate allowed Kathy to stay at 244 whenever she desired, telling Norah, "Now remember, Norah, always be good to Kathy. Do that for me, Norah."

Over the years, Norah and Kathy developed a mutual admiration for each other as well, and when Kate was away, the two of them spent a lot of time together. Mom loved the spark that Kathy exuded, while Kathy enjoyed Mom's own joie de vivre. Kathy tapped into a quality of Mom's that she couldn't really show to us kids; she appealed to the little girl in Norah.

They shared a passion for Irish culture; Kathy was involved with the Irish Repertory Theater, a group whose mission and productions were of utmost interest to Mom.

Pippa, Kathy's pet cat, who was kept under wraps at 244, played a part in their relationship. Kate was not a big fan of cats—she was more of a dog lover—so when the boss was around, Pippa spent most days upstairs behind closed doors. Often, just as Kate would close the door behind her when she left the house, Kathy would say to Norah, "When the cat's away, let's play!" Mom, enchanted by Kathy's impishness, was thrilled to join in. Like two little girls in a spirited chase, they would dash straight to the stairs and rescue Pippa from behind closed doors for a garden jaunt.

Pippa was not the only one Kathy took out to play. During the years that she lived at the brownstone, she'd often whisk Norah off to savor New

Kate's niece Katharine Houghton.

York City life. Together they fre-
quented Off-Broadway plays and
museums, and they would take
long meandering walks around
neighborhoods that were new to
Mom. Their topics of discussion
ranged from gossip to books and
practically everything in between.
Kate knew about the blossoming
friendship between her niece and
my mom—on more than one occasion, she declared, "Norah, Kathy
loves you more than me!" Norah
waved off the comment as silliness.

Kathy greatly enjoyed the company of my sister, Maureen, as well.
I remember the two of them setting
themselves up with an indoor pic-
nic of Kate's favorite chicken salad
with grapes, served on bed trays
that they'd eat off of as they gos-
siped up in Kathy's room. The two
would spend hours together eating
and chatting away. For Maureen,
Kathy was a great listener and

Norah and Katharine Houghton
in Kate's town house.

advice giver; for Kathy, Maureen was a fun and adoring little sister.

While Kathy was a big fan of Norah's and Maureen's, Kathy and I had
a bit of a rocky start. She met me when I was a teenager. That day I was in
high spirits, but they took a nosedive when I learned that Kate was due
back from her trip sooner than anticipated. Suddenly my early exit was
thwarted and my plans to go to an ice-skating party with friends were
ruined because Mom needed me all weekend. My mood swing—typical of

a fifteen-year-old—was not lost on Kathy. When Norah asked her opinion of me, she replied, "Well, she's either the queen or the corpse!" This character description, not unlike one Kate would have bestowed on someone prone to temper changes, became quite popular among my siblings, who still like to needle me with it from time to time. I'd like to believe that I've become much more even-keeled since then!

Kate's Friend
Laura Harding

Kate's personal life has long been and is still the topic of much intrigue and speculation. Female traveling companions, wearing pants, and living life on her terms led to innuendos about Kate's sexual preferences. Norah dismisses all kinds of rumors that inevitably surface when somebody famous attempts to lead a reclusive private life. Not unlike fellow iconic movie star Greta Garbo, Kate often wanted to be left alone.

But Kate did have a circle of close and devoted friends. Laura Harding, the American Express heiress, whom Kate met when they were both aspiring actresses, was Ms. Hepburn's friend for more than half a century. Though Laura never achieved the theatrical success of her pal, she was a very wealthy woman and enjoyed the many comforts that money offered her.

Mom met Laura Harding not long after she started working for Ms. Hepburn in the early 1970s. At that time it wasn't unusual for Miss Harding to drop in for lunch, even when Kate was off shooting a film somewhere. Two hundred forty-four East Forty-ninth Street was that type of place—people were always in and out of the kitchen. One day, Kate's

Kate with her close friend Laura Harding (at left).

younger brother, Dick, was also staying at the house. Happy to see his sister's old friend, he insisted that she join him for a lunch that Mom was busy preparing in the kitchen. When Dick asked Laura if she had any dietary restrictions or preferences, he was amused to learn that Miss Harding had a very particular dessert request: she wanted lemon gelatin. Dick thought that was a "hoot," as he put it—he was totally charmed that such an incredibly wealthy woman would have such simple taste in desserts.

But although Miss Harding liked uncomplicated sweets, her shopping preferences were anything but basic. Thanks to Laura, when Kate was out of town, Mom was introduced to all the fancy stores in New York City: Harry Winston, Saks Fifth Avenue, Bergdorf's, Barney's, Bloomingdale's— and more. Laura, who took her two dogs and Norah with her, would shop like crazy while Mom, the patient package holder, stood behind her. Inevitably, after a few days, and in one case, a month, Mom would get another call. "Norah, I need you!" Upon arriving at Ms. Harding's Sutton Place home, Norah would learn that Laura had had a change of heart about her purchases and wanted Mom to go back to those same stores and return most of what she'd bought. It's funny, but I think that Mom didn't mind it so much. In the end, Miss Harding offered her the chance to experience a world that was foreign and intriguing to her. The two always got on quite well.

Of course Kate was well aware of these shopping escapades, and she dismissed them as frivolous nonsense. Up until Miss Harding's death in 1994, Laura remained part of Kate's inner circle. The two old friends enjoyed spending hours and hours reminiscing about their years together.

Laura's Lemon Gelatin Dessert

• • •

SERVES 4

1 envelope Knox unflavored gelatin
½ cup cold water
⅓ cup granulated sugar
⅓ cup lemon juice
1 cup boiling water
1 tablespoon grated lemon rind
Pinch of salt
1 ripe banana, sliced

Stir the gelatin into the cold water. Mix in the sugar and lemon juice, followed by the boiling water and grated lemon rind. Add the salt and sliced banana and gently mix. Pour into individual serving cups, or a ceramic bowl, and refrigerate approximately 1 hour until set.

Spencer's Daughter

D espite the fact that Mom came on the Hepburn scene several years after Spencer had passed away, because Kate frequently talked about him—and was surrounded by his photos, clothing, and memorabilia—Mom felt a connection to the man with whom Katharine Hepburn shared a significant part of her life and her heart. So when Kate called to ask Norah to take Spencer's daughter, Susie Tracy, around the brownstone, Norah was honored to do so.

Kate was in London staying with friends during Susie's first visit to 244. "Susie's in town with her friend Ms. Moon. She's doing a showing of her prints." Kate beamed as she made her pronouncement. "She's a photographer, you know." Actually Mom did know, but she let her boss continue. "Have them over for dinner and do what you can." This was Kate-speak for *Make it as lovely as possible.*

Before dinner, Norah decided to take Susie and her friend on the grand tour of 244. The ever-appreciative Susie was quiet during the visit, but this gave Mom a chance to tell the tales she had been hearing for years.

"And this is your father in Rome among the catacombs," she indicated,

Norah with Spencer's daughter, Susie Tracy.

pointing at one of the many photos that lined the shelves in Kate's bed-room. "This is a medal that he gave Ms. Hepburn." Mom picked up the miraculous medal of Our Blessed Mother and let Susie run her fingers over it, before she gently replaced it. Norah couldn't help but notice the large gold cross that hung from a chain around Susie's neck.

They went into the bedroom next to Kate's, where Kate kept all of her clothes. There Susie could see Kate's sandals—all low heeled and neutral colored—alongside her hiking boots, lined up on a settee. Her characteris-tic turtlenecks—freshly washed and neatly folded—were, as Kate preferred them, laid out on the bed instead of in drawers or on shelves, as one might expect. The dresser housed items such as gloves and scarves, along with Kate's makeup: classic red lipstick and assorted eyeliners (she had a lot—and she kept them forever). Hats of all sizes and colors hung from every available edge of furniture. On the curtainless bar over the tub in the adjacent bathroom, they saw Kate's ironed pants and shirts hanging like soldiers in a row. When they entered Kate's private bathroom, Susie couldn't help but notice bottle after bottle of prescribed medicine, neatly lined up and obviously untouched. Norah saw her glance at them. "Oh, well, *you* know Ms. Hepburn," Mom said, realizing after she had said it that Susie really didn't know her. "She's pretty stubborn when it comes to taking medicine." Norah couldn't help but think that in that way, Kate wasn't unlike Spencer.

Susie glanced at a photo of Kate's mother. "Quite a looker, she was," Mom commented. Susie's eyes went to the wall that was covered with Hepburn family photos. She walked slowly, taking it all in. Then she noticed several ties hanging over the bathroom mirror. "Ah, those were your father's," Mom said as Susie gingerly lifted a couple to examine them. She gently held them in her palm before letting them fall back in place. "Ms. Hepburn calls these his Saint Paddy's Day ties." Susie smiled, clasped her hands together, and moved on. She stopped in front of Kate's dresser. There, standing by itself centered on top of two spotless pressed white linen doilies, was a silver-framed photograph of Spencer Tracy. The photo, taken at a slight angle, showed the profile of the ruggedly handsome actor. Mom couldn't help but comment, "He was quite a man." And then she opened the top drawer of Kate's dresser to show Susie something else: Spencer's old white pajamas, along with his flask.

So much was unsaid on that evening, yet it was clearly an icebreaker. That visit was the first of several that Susie Tracy made to 244. Later that night, Kate called to ask Mom how everything had gone. "She's a sweet girl," Mom said, referring affectionately to a woman who was clearly older than she. "We all had a lovely time." Norah could hear the sigh of relief in Kate's thank-you.

What's Left Unsaid

*I*n every close relationship there are ups and downs, and Norah and Kate's was no exception. The two women were equally set in their ways. As close as they were, Kate was always the employer, while Norah was always the employee, a dynamic that obviously influenced their connection.

In 1980, a year after my dad died, my mom, being a traditional Irish Catholic woman, arranged for an anniversary mass to be said for him at our local church. As custom dictated, she planned to open our home to thirty or forty family members and friends for a luncheon immediately following the service. My mom's plans did not conflict with work, since Kate was in Fenwick and wouldn't be returning for several days.

Sometimes my mom liked to keep things to herself. Though Kate had been an incredible help during my dad's illness, Mom decided she didn't want to bother her by telling her about her plans. Besides, Kate was never one for ceremony—the way she saw it, if you're gone, you're gone and the family should just privately move on.

A day before the event, Kate called Norah. "I need you to come in to 244 tomorrow and prepare dinner. Robert Helpmann and his friend are in

may god keep
you in his
loving care

the holy sacrifice
3 of the mass
will be offered
for your intentions,
with the sincere wishes of

*For Pat
with love
Katharine Hepburn*

KATHARINE HEPBURN
BY
Msgr. John J. Berlin

Kate's mass card for my father, Pat, who
was suffering from stomach cancer.

town and I must have them over." (Helpmann was a famous Australian Shakespearean actor and director with whom Kate had worked in the 1950s).

My mom, the loyal employee, acquiesced, never mentioning my dad's mass. She figured that she would get through the service, go back home, then leave the luncheon in the hands of her sisters.

The next day there was an unexpected snowstorm, so travel was neither as quick nor as easy as expected. Thanks to the help of friends who agreed to drive her into Manhattan, Norah arrived at 244 to find Kate and her secretary, Phyllis, already there at four, though they weren't due in until five. Mom had imagined the weather would have delayed their arrival as well.

Kate was visibly upset and began admonishing Norah for being late. My mother went through the motions of removing her coat, changing her shoes, and putting on her apron. But she was taken aback by Kate's behavior and comments, not to mention exhausted. Though my mother is a woman who manages to keep her emotions in check, this day was different. After a few more minutes, tears sprang into her eyes. Not wanting Kate to see her cry, Norah returned to the basement, where she kept her things. Exasperated, she started talking aloud to her late husband. "I've done nothing wrong! This is just too much!" she cried, working herself up instead of calming herself down.

Finally, she removed her apron, changed her shoes, picked up her coat, and headed back to the kitchen, where Kate, a bit baffled by Norah's behavior, was waiting. Norah proceeded to walk by her, coat on and pocketbook in hand. "I can't take it anymore," my mom announced as she headed toward the door.

Kate sprang up and grabbed Norah as she headed out. "Norah," she said as she held my mom's arm, "you have more character than that!"

Kate and my mother locked eyes, each firmly holding her ground. Finally, Kate released her hold, shook her head, and walked out of the room. Norah stood still for a moment. Then, as quickly as she'd come up the stairs, she turned around to head back down to leave her things. Within minutes, she was in the kitchen preparing the evening's dinner.

Though Norah and Kate never spoke of that day again, just over a week later Kate acknowledged the events by sending a very sweet note to our home, in which she asked, "What would I do without my Considine?"

Jane Fonda

*J*ane Fonda and Kate were both incredibly well known, talented, outspoken, intelligent, and beautiful.

Prior to the filming of *On Golden Pond*, in which Kate starred as Henry Fonda's wife, Jane came to the brownstone to meet Kate for the first time. Everyone knew that Jane's relationship with her dad was strained and that this film—one that in many ways mirrored real life—was especially important and poignant. So, according to Norah, Jane wanted to establish a friendship with Kate, someone whom she had admired her whole life.

The day they met, Jane, very considerately, had called earlier to ask if it was a good day to see her costar to be. Mom informed her that it would be a fine day for a visit as long as she came in the afternoon. Compliant, Jane had said she would be there later that day.

When Mom opened the door, she was immediately struck by Jane's elegance and beauty. Mom offered her a chair, and they started talking about this and that. Jane asked Mom about her roots. "Norah, my husband is Irish. And you're Irish too, aren't' you?" Mom was tickled by Jane's interest in her background. A little while later, Norah brought Jane up to see Kate.

After her visit with Jane that day, Kate came down to chat with Norah. "So, Norah dear, what did you think of Jane? You know her husband, Tom Hayden, he's some big political guy from California?"

Mom didn't know of Tom Hayden but in years to come would learn of his ten-year stint in the California State Assembly, as well as a bit about his and Jane's politics. For now she was just full of accolades for his wife. "Oh, yes, Ms. Hepburn, she's lovely. Her husband's Irish, she told me so herself.

Al Hirschfeld's caricature of the *On Golden Pond* cast.

Well, before she went upstairs, we were talking for a bit and I was thinking, you know, she looks Irish, too!"

According to Mom, Kate got a good chuckle out of that. (It's funny that somehow Norah always managed to find a bit of herself in everyone else, knowing that Kate enjoyed the company of Irish folks, too.)

The Flower Torrent

Katharine Hepburn's performances on Broadway in *West Side Waltz* coincided with an important milestone: my brother Patrick's wedding. During the run of the play in 1981, the Hepburn household was, as usual, filled with a flood of floral congratulations for Kate.

The flower deliveries peaked when news of the play's closing was announced, just before Patrick's wedding. Every time Norah turned around, there were more and more luscious bouquets arriving. Two hundred forty-four East Forty ninth Street became a virtual florist's shop, with flowers everywhere—even on the staircase.

Practical as ever, Kate had a solution. "Norah dear," she called when she arrived home and could barely move due to the gorgeous arrangements, which were now adorning every tabletop and floor space, "take these over to the church. Fischer," Kate summoned her driver, "have Norah give you the church address for Patrick's wedding and bring these over there." Soon the altar of the church was decorated with an abundance of floral delights.

But this was not the end of the flower torrent—more continued to arrive the next day. Mom had to think quickly. The church already had more than enough, and she couldn't leave them in the brownstone over the weekend. Like Kate, Norah wanted someone to enjoy them. Then she thought of a friend, a Franciscan brother who held services at St. Barnabas Church, in the Woodlawn section of the Bronx. This man had offered a great deal of comfort and solace to my mom during Dad's illness. Always thankful and appreciative of the support he had given her, my mother had kept in touch with him. She knew there were a lot of older parishioners in his church and thought they would enjoy the flowers' beauty.

Eyeing several *West Side Waltz* playbills on the settee, Norah had another idea. She went upstairs to Kate to tell her about the home she had found for the remaining bouquets. "Ms. Hepburn, I would love it if you could autograph these," she said, handing Kate the playbills, "so I can take them as well." Kate didn't like signing autographs, but for Norah she always made an exception.

Kate started signing them. But she couldn't resist asking a question.

Kate relaxing in her New York living room.

"Norah." She smiled, head down, still signing. "You are taking them to a church, no doubt?" Kate was well aware that Norah, like her beloved Spencer, was a devout Catholic.

"Yes, Ms. Hepburn," Norah responded, thanking her. With the help of Fischer, Mom placed the remaining flowers in the car and headed up to the Bronx. Upon arriving at St. Barnabas, Norah proudly sought out her friend to bring him to the car and show him the treats she was about to give him.

"My goodness," he remarked. "What's all this, Norah?"

"Well, you helped me when I was in need, and I'm eternally grateful. Now I'd like to give you these," Mom said.

Her appreciative friend helped Mom and Fischer unload the flowers from the car, and together they lovingly arranged them in the church. When the last of the bouquets was set, she handed Brother Brian Johnson a parting gift. Norah pulled out the autographed playbills and proudly said, "And these are from Katharine Hepburn." Overwhelmed with gratitude, Brother Brian thanked my mother, Fischer, and of course Ms. Hepburn, for all the gifts. As she and Fischer were leaving, my mom was sure to add, "Now make sure you say a prayer for her."

Barbara Walters

*L*ong before Barbara Walters hosted the television special that named Katharine Hepburn as one of the "100 Women of the Century," the pioneering talk-show host was a huge Hepburn fan. In the early 1980s, she became a frequent guest at 244 while preparing for her famous interview with Kate. After that interview, Walters was ridiculed for asking Kate the infamous question "If you could be a tree, what kind would it be?" Later, she was vindicated when it was revealed that in fact Kate had said she would want to be a tree, which prompted the interviewer's logical question.

The interview was done in stages during which the two women socialized both inside and outside Kate's home. They dined together on several occasions, and they went out together to see shows like the hit Broadway musical *Me and My Girl*. (Kate loved Robert Lindsey, the lead actor, so much that she went to see the musical five times.) Ms. Walters was around quite a bit during this period, and Mom got to know her—in a bit of a different light than the public.

Hilly, Kate's chauffeur at the time, considered himself quite familiar with Babs, as he affectionately called her in private. Hilly always watched her television interviews, and he told Mom that Ms. Walters seemed to be the same in real life as she was on television—she chose her words sparingly. He was in hysterics when, according to the conversation he overheard, Ms. Walters asked Kate if Spencer Tracy liked a particular dish. Hilly said Kate immediately retorted, "Oh, God, Barbara! Please. I can't even remember what *I* like to eat!"

During one afternoon session, the two women were chatting in the upstairs living room as they prepared for the filming that would take place in Kate's garden. Mom was downstairs when suddenly Kate summoned her with an ironing emergency. "Norah, I need you up here!" As soon as Mom reached the top step, Kate explained the problem. "Barbara just noticed a crease in the back of the dress she's going to wear during the interview that we're about to shoot outside—from the back." Kate gently

Kate's secretary, Phyllis Wilbourn, with Barbara Walters in Kate's town house.

lifted the dress and the hanger, then pulled the body of the dress toward them to point out the area that needed attention. Ms. Walters kept her head in her notes. Kate concluded, "Norah dear, see if you can get rid of that for her."

"I'll do my best," Mom said with a nod as she turned to head back downstairs. She noticed how gorgeous and expensive-looking the dress was.

As she descended, Mom could hear Kate reassuring Barbara, "Don't worry; Norah's the absolute *best*!" To which Norah didn't hear a response. No matter, she was on an ironing mission.

Norah went down to the old dark cellar, where the ironing board was permanently set up. She focused intensely on the task. That's what makes her so phenomenal at ironing, a skill I've yet to manage. As expected, Mom got rid of the ugly fold in the expensive fabric. Satisfied at last with her work, she hurried up to return the beautiful dress.

Quietly, not wanting to interrupt the interview, Mom went to hang up the garment from where Kate had plucked it. The two women were talking away, but Kate stopped and said she wanted to see it "Let's have a look," she pronounced, beckoning Norah to her. Norah of course obliged and was immediately thanked by Kate. "Yes, Norah. That's just perfect. Thank you!" Norah hung up the dress, turned, and received a broad smile from her boss but not a nod or a word from her boss's interviewer.

Martina Navrátilová

Tennis ranked high on Kate's list of passions, and Ms. Hepburn was one of Martina Navrátilová's favorite American actors. It seemed logical that the two would eventually meet and get along.

Kate and Martina's friendship began in the 1980s, at the height of the Czech tennis star's career. Martina subsequently became a frequent visitor to 244. At that time, Martina was with her long-time partner Judy Nelson, who usually joined her on these stops at Kate's.

My mom always speaks highly of Martina; she was one of Norah's favorite guests at the brownstone. Full of life and energy, Martina spent hours talking with Kate about many things, but it was tennis that Kate most enjoyed discussing with the athlete.

My mom appreciated Martina's down-to-earth style and generosity. Martina gave Norah tickets so that her sons, also big tennis fans, could attend the U.S. Open. Martina was genuinely interested in everyone at 244, and even stopped to take pictures with Kate's handyman at the time, Dennis Lynch. Norah also admired Martina's attitude when it came to food. Norah knew that Martina's trainer had her on a very strict regimen—while she was in training, she couldn't even eat a grape because of the sugar content! Martina was probably the only guest who was ever on such a strict diet, but she never made a fuss; without exception, she ate whatever Norah was serving. Mom boasts that it was incredibly rare for her to pick up a plate at 244 that still held any food!

After Martina won Wimbledon in 1983, she came to New York for a visit. Kate was excited. She had pored over details of the matches in the *New York Times* sports section—Kate didn't own a television until a couple of years later!—and she couldn't wait to congratulate Martina over dinner at 244.

The night that Martina dined with Kate, after the last course was served and the dishes were cleared, Martina presented her winning racquet to her dear friend. Kate, needless to say, was thrilled. Mom always says, "Such a nice girl, that Martina."

From left, Martina's partner Judy Nelson, Norah, and Martina.

Cynthia McFadden

ecause she had such a spark, Kate was able to identify a spark in others. When she met Cynthia McFadden in the early 1980s—years before Cynthia became a world-famous news correspondent—Kate was immediately taken with her, finding her to be a lot of fun, easy to be with, and smart. At the time a law student at Columbia University, Cynthia grew to be very close to Ms. Hepburn—even living for a couple of years on the fourth floor of the brownstone. (Kate later named Cynthia the executor of her estate, along with Erik Hansen.) The first wedding ever to be held at Fenwick was Cynthia McFadden's, to Michael Davies, in 1989, and the correspondent later named her son after Kate's great love: Spencer.

Cynthia was full of life and very direct, not unlike Kate herself. Kate must have seen something of herself in Cynthia; she always said Cynthia had *it*—that elusive star quality that made her stand out in a crowd.

My mom tells a story about Cynthia that illustrates the kind of relationship Cynthia and Kate had. Like Kate, Cynthia loved nature and visits to Fenwick. On one weekend at the estate, the two friends went flower picking during a morning stroll. Upon returning to the house, Cynthia wanted to arrange her floral collection. She pulled out one of Kate's many vases and started working on the placement of the flowers. She was unaware that Kate was closely watching her. The actress critically observed her young friend for a few moments before commenting, "No, Cynthia! That's not right." Ms. Hepburn walked over to the vase and started reorganizing. "You do it like this, see?" Hands at her side, Cynthia watched with amusement as Kate yanked and tugged at the poor stems until at last she seemed satisfied. Stepping aside to inspect her handiwork, Kate turned to her young friend and said, "Now that's how it's done!"

"Well," said Cynthia, totally unfazed by Kate's remarks, "I can't be great in *every* room!"

With that, Kate laughed and let Cynthia finish the arrangement herself.

Kate's friend Cynthia McFadden.

Fenwick Meat Loaf

A famous staple in Katharine Hepburn's kitchens was Mom's meat loaf. Kate just loved it! Kate being Kate, she cherished serving her guests foods that she especially enjoyed. Norah would frequently prepare this dish with meat always bought at Jack's, a now-defunct butcher shop on Second Avenue between Forty-ninth and Fiftieth streets. (After Jack's closed, they always bought meat at Walt's Food Mart in Old Saybrook and brought it back to 244!) When Mom was in New York, and Kate was heading up to Fenwick, she would often send Ms. Hepburn off with a fresh warm loaf.

•   •   •

SERVES 10

1 pound ground beef
1 pound ground pork
1 pound ground veal
1 cup Pepperidge Farm bread crumbs
½ cup beef bouillon
½ cup Parmesan cheese
2 large eggs
1 onion, chopped
1 teaspoon minced garlic
Salt and pepper to taste
Additional herbs or spices to taste
Olive oil for greasing the pan
¾ cup chopped fresh parsley

Preheat the oven to 350° F. In a large bowl, combine the meats, bread crumbs, bouillon, and cheese. Stir in the eggs and onion. Add the garlic and salt and pepper, along with any other herbs or spices. Place the mixture in a large greased loaf pan and make a deep horizontal indent along the top of the loaf. Sprinkle the parsley into the cut. Bake in the preheated oven for 1 hour. Serve immediately. (Kate liked all of her cooked food served piping hot.)

The Missing Madonna and Child

During the thirty years that Mom worked for Katharine Hepburn, she was always coming home with things ranging from usable goods like books, scarves, photos, and chocolates to questionable ones like red flannel sheets and statues. We took these items for granted and looked at them as things that Mom's boss was discarding.

One Saturday morning in the early 1980s, Mom came downstairs in a bit of a panic. She asked the five of us kids, "Does any one of you know where that statue is?" She was serious, and her voice was tinged with displeasure. Since most of us were teenagers, we reacted in our sullen, nonchalant manner.

This got Mom even more agitated. "I'm talking about the Madonna and child statue—the wooden one I brought home several months ago!" Norah was getting impatient. She directed her next question to me. "Did you do anything with it, Eileen?"

I resented her accusatory tone, but I did remember something about a statue, and said, "Ugh, that old thing?" Mom started showing signs of being very fed up with all of us. "I think it's down in the basement somewhere,"

I continued as I stuck my hand in a box of Cap'n Crunch cereal. "Well, you're always asking us to try and keep things tidy. I couldn't find a place for it, and besides, it doesn't go with anything in our living room."

By this time Mom was so upset about the missing piece, she didn't care about my digging my hand into the family's cereal supply as I sat atop the kitchen counter. She walked over to me, looked me in the eye, and continued her questioning, not seeming to notice as my siblings quietly exited the room one by one.

"Please don't tell me you threw it down there with all that old junk! Is it in the back room? What did you do with it?" Her face was now completely flushed, and as nonchalant as I had been, I began to feel as if I had made a horrible mistake.

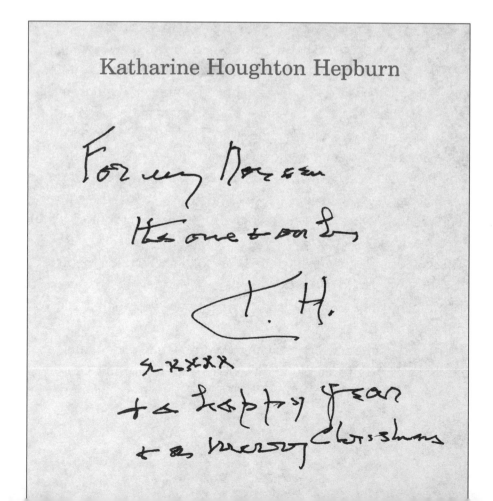

This must have shown, because Mom softened her tone a bit. "Really, Eileen. You should have asked me about it first."

I muttered, "I'm sorry," and pulled my hand out of the cereal box. Mom continued, "I shouldn't have to account for things in my own home. Don't you know that piece is very special to me?" She didn't wait for my answer but continued with an explanation. "Ms. Hepburn gave it to me—and let me tell you what she said: 'Here, Norah, take this. It was Spencer's. It sat on his bedside table during all our years together in our little house in California. Keep it,' she said. 'You're my only Catholic friend.'"

Mom's back was now to me. Her hands were resting on the kitchen table. Though I couldn't see her eyes, I knew they were misty. I felt horrible.

I hopped off the counter, put my arm around my mother, and encouraged her to join me in the basement to find the statue.

We found it all right, and although it was a bit dusty, it was in one piece. It looked different to me; hearing Mom's story made it seem much more special.

Maybe that's why I was a bit surprised years later when Mom told me she was going to give it away—but then when she told me to whom I understood. She decided to donate it to the St. Joseph's House for the Adult Deaf and Deaf/Blind in Ireland in honor of Spencer Tracy, who had cherished not only the statue but also his beloved son, John, who was deaf.

Publicity photograph.

Publicity photograph.

Cary Grant and Kate in *Bringing Up Baby*.

Kate lighting James Stewart's cigarette in *The Philadelphia Story*.

Kate's living room in Fenwick, Connecticut.

Kate's library in her Forty-ninth Street New York town house.

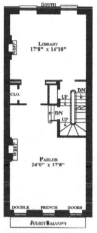

244 EAST 49TH STREET

GARDEN LEVEL & PARLOR FLOOR

Garden Level:

GATE TO COMMUNAL GARDEN

SOUTH FACING GARDEN
41'6" x 19'0"

TREE

STATUE

DINING ROOM
17'8" x 15'0"

WBFP

PANTRY

TO CELLAR

CL.

EAT-IN KITCHEN
21'10" x 11'2

REF.

ENTRY HALL
25' x 6'

UP

DW

SERVICE NORTH   **ENTRY**

GARDEN LEVEL

Parlor Floor:

SOUTH

LIBRARY
17'8" x 14'10"

WBFP

CLO.

UP   DN

DN   UP

UP

WBFP

PARLOR
24'0" x 17'8"

DOUBLE FRENCH DOORS

JULIET BALCONY

PARLOR FLOOR

The first two floors of Kate's Turtle Bay town house.

Kate's New York living room.

Kate with Vanessa Redgrave in the
1971 film *The Trojan Women*.

Photo taken during the filming of *The Glass Menagerie*, 1973.

Norah and Kate, holding firewood, in front of Kate's New York town house in January 1979.

Title	Year Released
Bill of Divorcement	1932
Morning Glory	1933
Little Women	1933
Christopher Strong	1933
Little Minister	1934
Spitfire	1934
Alice Adams	1935
Break of Hearts	1935
A Woman Rebels	1936
Mary of Scotland	1936
Sylvia Scarlett	1936
Quality Street	1937
Stage Door	1937
Holiday	1938
Bringing Up Baby	1938
Philadelphia Story	1940
Woman of The Year	1942
Keeper of The Flame	1942
Dragon Seed	1944
Without Love	1945
Undercurrent	1946
Song of Love	1947
State of The Union	1948
Adam's Rib	1949

stage door Canteen

African Queen	1951
Pat & Mike	1952
Summertime	1955
The Rainmaker	1956
Desk Set	1957

the 9pm Petticoat
suddenly last summer

Long Day's Journey Into Night	1962
Guess Who's Coming to Dinner?	1967
Lion in Winter	1968

madwoman of Chaillot
Trojan Women

Dick Cavett Interview *Glass Menagerie*	1973
Rooster Cogburn	1975
Love Among The Ruins *Ollie Ollie Ofen*	1975
A Delicate Balance	
60-Minutes Interview	1979
The Corn Is Green (video)	1979
On Golden Pond	1981

the Ultimate solution of grace. quigley   19
1983

List of Kate's films through 1983 as compiled by her secretary Phyllis.

Photograph inscribed to my brother Joe on his birthday.

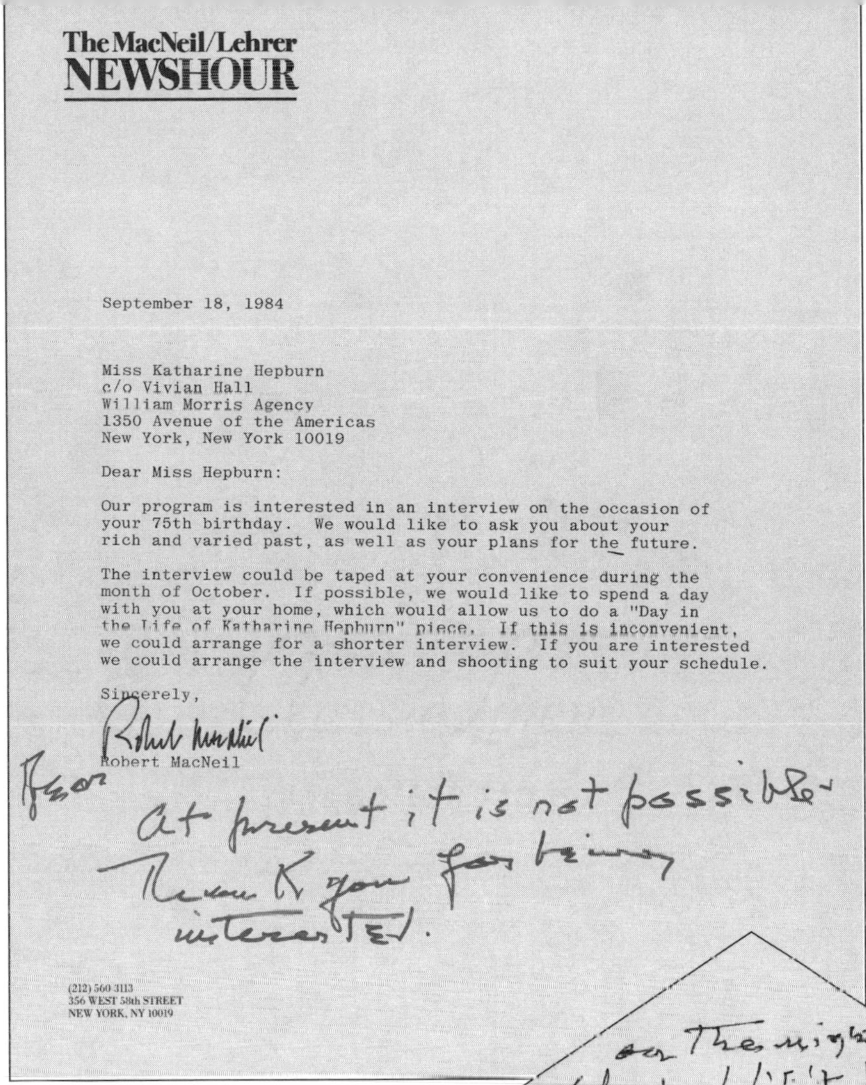

The MacNeil/Lehrer NEWSHOUR

September 18, 1984

Miss Katharine Hepburn
c/o Vivian Hall
William Morris Agency
1350 Avenue of the Americas
New York, New York 10019

Dear Miss Hepburn:

Our program is interested in an interview on the occasion of your 75th birthday. We would like to ask you about your rich and varied past, as well as your plans for the future.

The interview could be taped at your convenience during the month of October. If possible, we would like to spend a day with you at your home, which would allow us to do a "Day in the Life of Katharine Hepburn" piece. If this is inconvenient, we could arrange for a shorter interview. If you are interested we could arrange the interview and shooting to suit your schedule.

Sincerely,

Robert MacNeil

Robert MacNeil

Dear
At present it is not possible—
Thank you for being
interested.

(212) 560-3113
356 WEST 58th STREET
NEW YORK, NY 10019

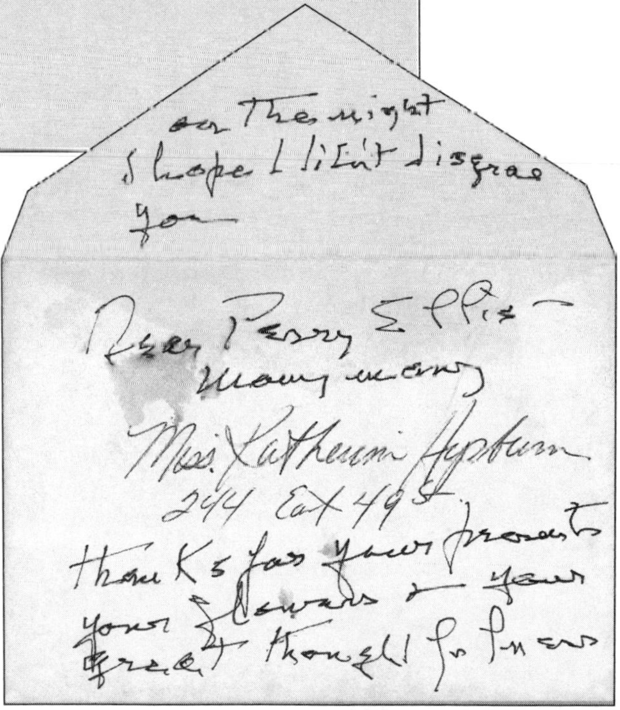

on the night
I hope I didn't disgrace
you
Dear Perry Ellis—
Many many
Miss Katharine Hepburn
244 East 49 St
thanks for your presents
your flowers & your
great thought for [illegible]

Envelope with note to fashion legend Perry Ellis.

Saint Patrick's Day

Every year, just a few days before the beginning of spring, Kate would get ready to head up to Fenwick. She would leave 244 to Norah, who would get ready to play hostess for her own soirée for her favorite holiday, Saint Patrick's Day, of course. Friends and relatives of Mom's would travel from near and far to New York City for the parade and Norah's annual party. Mom's annual St. Paddy's Day party drew more than a hundred guests.

Though Kate could have attended, she preferred to enjoy the party vicariously through Mom. "Norah," Kate would begin in the first week of March, "you and your gang can have the house again—and have some fun!" Kate knew Norah planned to make tons of food and have her crowd over. She also knew that Norah would have plenty of helpers and that nothing in the house would be disrupted. There were no invitations, and according to true Irish custom friends of friends were always welcome. These parties always included a very large family called the O'Deas, whose grandmotherly matriarch, Mary O'Dea, was considered by Norah to be her mother in America.

The party had its own traditions. In addition to musicians and dancers, there were contests. The "Rose of Tralee" was not only a song they played but also a contest that the women prepared for. Judged on their beauty, grace, and personality, they would wear specially made gowns, similar to the ones they and their ancestors had worn in contests held in Ireland for well over a century. In this case, the wardrobe was provided by Kate, who was happy for Mom and her friends to take the clothing worn on one movie set or another out of storage and put it to good use! With accompanying traditional Irish music, they restaged the event just as they had done it in their home country, the women dancing around to the thunderous applause of the observers. The winner, chosen by John James, Mary O'Dea's

Norah, with crown, at one of her famous St. Patrick's Day parties.

son-in-law, would hand out the crown to the winning woman. Of course Mom had her chance—more than once—to be Rose of Tralee for a day.

When Kate returned to the brownstone, she'd find it just as tidy as it had been when she left, and she'd ask Norah to share her St. Paddy's Day photos. "What a fun group," she'd say, looking at the bunch of dancing and singing Irish folk. Kate loved details, and she'd ask Mom about the people in the pictures; she'd stare at the faces in the photos and listen as Mom vividly recounted the events of the day. After going through the photos, Kate unfailingly made the same comment: "Norah, they're always welcome here." And she meant it.

Irish Soda Bread

This recipe, created by one of Norah's cousins back in Ireland, became a staple for 244 party guests as soon as it was introduced. Best served hot out of the oven, this bread can also be frozen for future toasting and eating.

•   •   •

MAKES 1 LOAF
OF ABOUT
14 SLICES

4 cups unbleached flour, plus additional for dusting a cutting board

4 teaspoons baking powder

1 cup granulated sugar

2 cups raisins

4 teaspoons caraway seeds

4 eggs

1 pint sour cream

1 teaspoon baking soda

1½ sticks salted butter, plus additional for greasing the pan

Preheat the oven to 375° F. In a large mixing bowl, combine the flour, baking powder, sugar, raisins, and caraway seeds and set aside.

In a small bowl, combine the eggs, sour cream, and baking soda and mix well. Slowly add this liquid mixture to the dry ingredients.

Lightly dust a wooden cutting board with flour. Place the dough on it and gently roll it back and forth in order to shape it into a loaf. Transfer the loaf to a greased 2-quart baking pan and bake for 1 hour.

Kate, Norah, and Money

As reasonable and just as Katharine Hepburn was, she was certainly not delicate when it came to expressing her opinion. We all learned this right from the start. As a teenager, I was often taken aback by her roughness of tongue combined with her incredible sense of fairness; the two just didn't seem to match. However, looking back now—if only I knew then what I know now! —I respect more than ever Ms. Hepburn's candor. I am also eternally grateful for her support of me; the great Kate sometimes understood things Mom didn't.

One morning in the early 1980s, when Mom arrived at work, she found two envelopes on the kitchen table with her daughters' names printed on them. Both Maureen and I had worked at a party at the brownstone the previous evening, helping Mom, who was working as usual in the kitchen. Without opening the envelopes, Mom knew what they contained.

"That wasn't necessary, Ms. Hepburn," Mom pronounced, pointing to the envelopes as her boss entered the room.

Kate didn't miss a beat. "You don't care about money," she said to

Norah, "but your daughters and sisters will!" Mom's sisters also joined the workforce at 244 on occasion.

Mom reluctantly pocketed the envelopes, which she gave us later that evening. "Take this, Eileen. I'm guessing it's a check for the party you worked." Mom sat down and sighed. She wasn't done expressing herself on the issue. "Actually, Eileen, don't tell me what's in it. I don't want to know!" Of course she knew, but Mom—being Mom—felt she had to say that. And then came the guilt trip. "You know, Eileen, you shouldn't take it," she continued as she watched me gleefully pull out the typed-out check that Kate's secretary had prepared for me. "After all, Ms. Hepburn's been so good to you already."

But Mom's words fell on deaf ears—there was no way I was going to not take the check! I had earned that money and Kate knew it. As I picked up the envelope and was about to exit the room, I noticed a note, addressed to Maureen and me, that I hadn't seen before. I had to share it with Mom.

"Well, Mom," I said smugly, sneaking a look over at her, "you're right— it's a check. But look here." I couldn't hide my glee. "There's a note about you!"

Mom took the letter out of my hand. After a moment she shook her head with a bemused smile. "Oh, go on, Eileen. Read it aloud to the boys; I'm sure they'll enjoy hearing it, too." Obediently, I read the note:

> Dear Maureen and Eileen,
>
> You were angels and looked so pretty and made it so easy. Thank you very much.
>
> Katharine Hepburn
>
> P.S. Don't tell your mother: she doesn't approve of money.

The bunch of us had a good laugh.

As seriously as Mom held to her convictions, she never lost her sense of humor—and she always appreciated Kate's.

Discoveries

As soon as Kate was scheduled to return home from a trip, Mom would call in the recruits for assistance at 244 East Forty-ninth Street. I was one of the principal members of her team. As teenager, I was often reluctant to leave the comforts of television and friends to head from the Bronx into exotic Manhattan, but I knew the day would offer me more than just monetary benefits. Working at Kate's was hard, but it was also entertaining—it offered insight into the life of Mom's boss, who to me was an incredibly fascinating woman.

One day Mom had installed me on the fourth floor of the brownstone in a rarely used bedroom down the hall from where Kate's guests stayed. She had given me a bucket filled with Murphy's Oil Soap and water, gloves, and sponges, as well as the parameters of my cleaning territory. Before leaving, she said, "And don't forget to clean behind the door!"

"Okay, okay," I mumbled as I struggled with the rubber gloves.

Mom continued, "Now, Eileen, I'm leaving you to your own devices." Her voice grew softer as she headed down the stairs. "But if you need something, just give me a shout!"

244 EAST 49TH STREET

THIRD AND FOURTH FLOORS

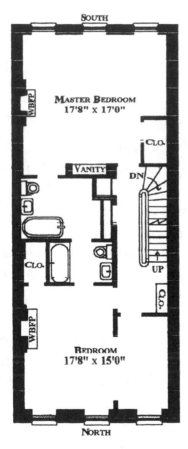

THIRD FLOOR

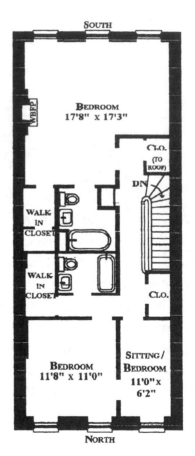

FOURTH FLOOR

Floor plans of the third and fourth floors of Kate's town house.

Typical, I thought. She leaves me to my own devices, but then she tells me what to do.

I started scrubbing the floor. Amazing how dirty a wood floor could get even when nobody was walking on it. I was on my hands and knees, making good progress, when I heard Mom coming up the stairs again.

"Oh, Eileen," she started, her voice now increasing in volume as she approached. "I almost forgot." She came into the room and pointed behind the door.

"Mom, I got it! Behind the door!" I retorted in my know-it-all manner. Then something caught my eye.

Mom ignored my tone. "You see those soldiers there?" she said. I walked over to see four glittering figures, one right after another, resting behind the door.

"Mom!" I exclaimed in awe as I realized what I was looking at.

"Yes, those are Ms. Hepburn's Oscar statues. They've been tucked away behind this door for years," Mom said in a tone of admiration mixed with disbelief. "Hard to believe, Eileen. But that's where she keeps them. Out of sight . . . "

Mom shook her head and left me there. I couldn't help but pick up the figures. After having only seen Oscars on television, they hardly seemed real.

A couple of years later, I was all the way upstairs, in the hallway near Kate's bedroom. Mom had given me specific instructions to dust the glass shelves, which were jam-packed with all kinds of knickknacks, photos, and memorabilia. To reach the high shelves, I needed a ladder. So there I was, feather duster in hand, working my way across the top shelf, when I came across a big round jar. I couldn't see what was inside because of a hazy, thick liquid on the jar's side.

Hmmm, I thought. What in the world is this? I knew my mom would disapprove of my prying where I shouldn't—she was always worried that

I'd break something of Kate's, not to mention the fact that she didn't like me looking into her boss's stuff—but I was curious. I glanced around quickly, stepped off the ladder, put the duster down, and proceeded to twist open the mysterious jar.

Luckily I wasn't on the ladder because the smell of formaldehyde that came wafting up nearly knocked me off my feet. I quickly screwed the top back on and stepped up on the ladder to replace the jar. Then, as if my mom had radar, she came up the stairs.

"How's it going, Eileen?" I muttered an okay and then glanced toward the jar. "You don't need to touch that," Mom said. "Can't you see the bone inside?" I felt a bit of nausea creeping up my throat. Mom continued, "That's Kate's hip bone, so be careful."

Years later, Kate gave her jarred hip bone to Mom. "She wanted me to have it," she pronounced when I looked surprised.

Eventually Norah took the hip bone to Kate sister Peg's house; Mom felt the bone should stay with the family.

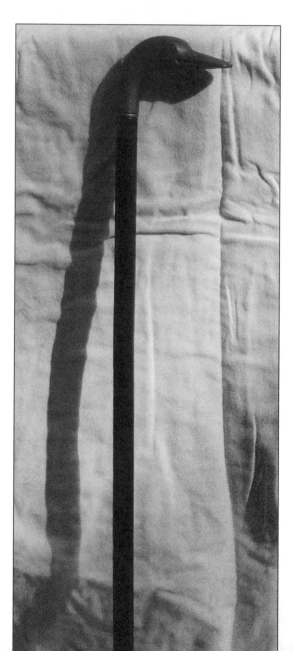

Kate's walking stick.

The Handyman

ike her boss, Mom always greeted everyone from the UPS guy to the garbagemen with the same enthusiasm; both Kate and Norah had the utmost respect for workingmen and workingwomen. Perhaps it was this respect that helped them find assistance on the rare occasions when they couldn't handle something themselves.

Mom met Dennis Lynch, the superintendent from across the street, a few years after she started working at 244 East Forty-ninth Street. Kate had mentioned the handyman several times; she was impressed by his talent and his great sense of humor.

On one occasion, when Kate had been given tickets to see the Broadway play *42nd Street* and couldn't make it, and Norah was busy as well, they decided to offer them to someone they thought would really appreciate them: Dennis. That's how Mom and Dennis became friends.

After that, Mom called on Dennis when there was something Kate and she couldn't handle. Dennis always put on a grudging air, but he was obviously very happy to help the ladies out, especially because he was, like so many others, a huge fan of Mom's culinary capabilities. It didn't take long before the handyman from across the way became a regular visitor to 244.

Dennis always had a funny comment for us all. One day, Mom needed a buzzer in Kate's house fixed, so, as usual, she called her friend.

"Dennis? Dennis Lynch?" Norah asked when he picked up the phone. As soon as she heard his gruff voice, she continued, "Oh, good! You're there. I need a favor. Can you come over quick?"

Norah's sweet voice was the antithesis of Dennis's—but a good part of his roughness was bravado. "Don't tell me you're calling again about your old rookery across the way?" he admonished. "There's always something breaking down in that house. And besides, I'm busy! Don't forget, I have my own building to run."

Mom continued as if he had said he'd be right over. "Dennis dear," she said in her melodious voice, "I've got some lovely soup—not to mention the brownies with nuts. Why, I know those are your favorite." Mom couldn't resist continuing, "And they smell so good; they're just out of the oven."

In less than five minutes, Dennis was at the door. He entered, his eyes focused on the soup and brownies, but Mom quickly took him by the hand. "Ah, Dennis, you're a good friend," she cooed as she brought him into the dining room and toward Kate's table, a reproduction of the dining room table on the *Mayflower*.

"Now here's the problem," Mom said, lifting the rug and exposing a button on the floor. "You see, Kate sits right here," she pointed to a chair and indicated that Dennis should bend down to check out the floor. "Whenever she needs something, she just taps this button with her foot and a light goes on in the pantry and I hear a gentle ringing. But now it's not working. Can you fix it for me, Dennis?"

So there was Dennis on his hands and knees while Mom held the rug back. She looked down at him as he examined the wires surrounding the area. He shook his head as he looked up at her.

"For this you called me over?" he asked, half smiling as he stood up. "Ah, Norah. Surely this bell's not necessary." A smile started to creep across his face as he looked at Mom. "Isn't *she* easy enough to hear?"

"Oh, stop," Mom said with a smile as she waved off his joke. "Come, I'll feed you first!" As usual, Mom made everyone happy: Kate got her bell back and Dennis, as always, got his treats.

Kate's Brownies

Mom never ceased to be amazed at how a woman who loved sweets so much managed to stay so thin! Kate adored all kinds of sweets; her absolute favorite was ice cream, but brownies with walnuts, made following a Hepburn family recipe, were certainly one of her top choices. Norah was constantly making trays of them—and we were always forced into the act. I remember a time when I was so tired of chopping walnuts into bite-size pieces that any time someone started raving about Mom's chocolate treats I'd be filled with dread! I even stopped eating them for a while just so I wouldn't be pulled back into walnut chopping. Kate's recipe called for a quarter cup or a tablespoon of flour or none at all, but Mom usually added a tablespoon. Kate requested that Norah keep these on hand to serve at home and to be ready to be packed up in tins to give to friends.

•   •   •

MAKES ABOUT
16 BROWNIES

2 eggs at room temperature
¼ pound sweet butter
2 squares Baker's chocolate (unsweetened)
1 cup granulated (regular white) sugar
Pinch of salt
½ teaspoon vanilla
1 cup roughly chopped walnuts
1 tablespoon flour

Preheat the oven to 325° F. In a medium saucepan over low heat, melt the butter and chocolate together until smooth. Transfer to a mixing bowl.

With a wooden spoon, add the sugar and salt and blend. In a cup, beat the eggs with the vanilla, then pour the mixture into the mixing bowl. Stir in the chopped walnuts. Add a big rounded tablespoon of flour and blend it in. Beat this mixture as hard as you can; if you find it is too limp, you can add up to a tablespoon more flour. Pour the mixture immediately into a greased pan and quickly place the pan in the hot oven. Bake for 40 minutes. When the brownies are cool, cut them into 1-inch squares.

Maureen's Big News

My sister's pregnancy was not a welcome surprise. At the time, Maureen was just twenty-two years old and still living at home. Though it had been five years since Dad had passed away, things were still a bit rough: Norah was working ten hours a day for Kate, from 10 A.M. to 8 P.M., my eldest brother had recently gotten married and moved out, and Maureen, well, Maureen was a bit wild and not getting along too well with Mom. Furthermore, the father of the child, who was as young as Maureen was, was clearly not going to stay in the picture. While Norah did dream of having grandchildren, this was not the way she had imagined it would happen. Besides, Norah always wanted more for her kids; now she felt as if she had failed her daughter.

For the next three months, Norah kept the news a big secret, but the burden of Maureen's pregnancy affected my mom every day. As usual, she worked, but she just went through the motions.

Kate had been traveling a great deal during Maureen's first few months of pregnancy, so she hadn't yet caught on to my mom's altered demeanor. "Norah, what's going on with you?" Kate asked one day upon returning from a trip, entering the kitchen and finding her normally focused helper a bit distracted. "Don't you have any Irish jokes for me?" she cajoled. Norah was simply not in the mood. Kate persisted.

"Come here," Kate beckoned. "What's the matter with you? Norah, what the hell is wrong?" Kate asked as she grabbed my mom's arms.

My mom, exhausted from keeping the news in, suddenly burst into tears. "Let's sit, Norah," Kate said as she brought my mother over to the small table and chairs.

Norah poured out the news to her boss. She confessed her embarrassment and guilt. "How could I have let this happen?" she asked as Kate pushed a box of tissues toward her.

Kate listened to Mom's story and let her cry just a bit. Then, as if signaling the end of the outpouring, she tapped the table with the palm of her hand.

"Norah, now *stop* that," Kate commanded in a rough yet understanding tone. "It's past. Besides," she started, softening up a bit, "the child will be good for Maureen. It will give her stability."

Just talking about my sister's pregnancy with Kate made a big difference to my mom, for though she still had trouble dealing with it, the initial shock passed. In fact, it became a regular topic of conversation. Kate always asked how Maureen was doing, and Mom was happy to report everything from Maureen's appetite to the baby's kicks.

When her first grandchild was born, my mother was excited to call Kate and tell her the news. "Well, Ms. Hepburn, I've got another girl!" Kate was equally thrilled. "Congratulations! That's great, Norah dear," she responded.

When Norah next reported for work at 244 East Forty-ninth, Kate greeted her with a hug. She handed Norah a black-and-white photograph of a mother and baby giraffe walking in the wilds of Africa, a note of congratulations, and a generous check for Maureen. Norah had seen the photo in Kate's bedroom and always thought Kate had brought the

picture back after she completed the film *The African Queen*. Kate took Mom's hands in hers and said in a demanding yet gentle way that if she ever needed *anything*, she should let her know. "And you tell that to Maureen, too," she added, squeezing Mom's hand and looking deeply into her teary eyes.

Stephen Sondheim, the Technician

Though Stephen Sondheim—one of the most important figures in contemporary musical theater—was not the most visible neighbor of Kate's, Mr. Sondheim did help Kate out with a technical hitch on one occasion.

One day in the mid-1980s, Kate received a package from her grandniece, the actress Schuyler Grant. Schuyler had sent a VHS tape of her commercial work to be seen by all at 244. Kate was delighted and excitedly began talking about Schuyler and her budding career. She turned to my sister, Maureen, who was helping out that day, and to my mom and asked them to join her upstairs to watch it. Mom, who was busy in the kitchen, declined, saying she had too much to do, but Maureen followed Kate upstairs. Although Kate never watched TV, she had received not long before a state-of-the-art entertainment center (which included a VCR) as a gift from some of her producer friends, so Kate and Maureen attempted to figure out how to watch the tape. Apparently there were three remotes attached to the side of the television, but neither Kate nor Maureen could figure out how to turn on the television.

"Norah," Kate bellowed down to Mom, "can you fix this nonsense?"

Norah at Kate's neighbor Stephen Sondheim's harpsichord, which his mother turned into a desk.

Mom was as technically challenged as Kate, but she had her connections. Mom told my sister to run next door to get help from Louis, Mr. Sondheim's chef.

Maureen did as mother instructed and knocked on the kitchen window next door. Inside she saw Louis, who called her in. Maureen explained the dilemma she and Kate were having. Stephen Sondheim had overheard her tale, and he walked into the room to offer his assistance. "I know how they work; I'll come over and see what I can do," he said before following Maureen next door.

Stephen and Maureen walked upstairs. Kate, who was sitting on the couch, turned toward Stephen. "Hello, Ms. Hepburn," he said before approaching the entertainment center. He went directly to the mechanism on the back of the TV and got the tape going in no time (they hadn't turned the switch from television to VCR). He declined the offer to join the ladies on the couch but he did stay to watch the tape; prior to leaving he commented that he thought Schuyler was quite talented.

Kate never did become mechanically inclined, but she enjoyed several of her talented neighbor's recipes thanks to exchanges between Louis and Mom. This recipe for gazpacho, an interpretation of the traditional chilled Spanish vegetable soup, was one of Stephen's favorites and one that Mom included her in repertoire, both in Manhattan and up in Fenwick.

Stephen Sondheim's Gazpacho

• • •

SERVES 6 TO 8

1 or 2 cloves garlic (or to taste)
1 medium red onion, coarsely chopped
¼ cup olive or vegetable oil
2 tablespoons red wine vinegar
One 8-ounce can V-8 tomato juice
Salt and pepper to taste
2 pounds ripe Italian tomatoes, peeled and coarsely chopped
1 medium unpeeled cucumber, coarsely chopped
One 8-ounce can Campbell's beef bouillon
Tabasco to taste
1 cup ice cubes

In a blender, combine the garlic, onion, oil, vinegar, V-8, and salt and pepper and process until smooth. Add the tomatoes, cucumber, beef bouillon, and Tabasco and process. Strain into a large bowl. Add the ice cubes. Cover and refrigerate to chill (at least 1 hour) and then serve, or keep for up to 1 week.

STEPHEN SONDHEIM

November 7, 1987

Dear Norah –

Thank you so much for the wire and the terrific soda bread. They both helped make the opening day and night a terrific experience.

Gratefully,

Steve S.

Entertaining Molly

Mom's list of responsibilities at 244 East Forty ninth Street included being the gatekeeper—the flow of fans was constant. It was often up to Norah to dismiss or accept the adoring members of Kate's ever-increasing fan base. Over the course of the years, there were several fans to whom Norah, for varying reasons, would take a shine. Often Norah succumbed and made introductions, pretending that the fans were visiting relations of hers. Once, when Kate had just about reached her limit with Mom's "relatives," she demanded, "My word, Norah! How many cousins do you have?"

Norah so often found people waiting outside the brownstone for a glimpse of their idol, that when she told us about the two kids from Canada, we, her own set of teens, didn't bat an eye. We actually thought they must have been nuts! The fans waited across the street for two days in the pouring rain. On the third day, one of them sheepishly came to the door and asked for an autograph. Mom, who admired their tenacity and was certainly a sucker for helping out cold, wet teenagers, brought them both in, gave them some hot tea, and then gave them a much-awaited introduction to Kate. I imagine it had been a very slow day at 244! Kate learned that they had traveled all the way to Manhattan during their school vacation in the hope of meeting her. Not only were their dreams realized, Norah still keeps in touch with one of them.

Of all the fans that Norah befriended, the most entertaining was Molly. Often clothed in the remnants of beautiful furs, fine jewelry, and attractive clothes, the fiftysomething woman had a certain elegance. She had been kept by a wealthy man for years until he passed away. She was kind of a peripheral fan; she'd arrive at Kate's under the assumption that she was an invited guest.

Molly lived nearby in a tiny apartment over a Chinese restaurant. Mom learned all about Molly's situation: she lived alone, had no family, and had no real source of income. Norah felt sorry for Molly, who, though she was sometimes confused as to where she should go (or where she shouldn't go), had plenty of tales to tell, from contracting tuberculosis in her early twenties and almost dying in a hospital in Saranac Lake (her aunt had even picked out her coffin), to being a high-class call girl, living a life filled with fine dining, dancing, and a long list of crazy characters.

One time, while Kate was alone upstairs, she heard Molly chatting away with Mom in the kitchen.

"Norah," Kate called from her living room. "Who are you talking to?"

"Oh, I'm with my friend Molly, Ms. Hepburn."

Without even knowing who Molly was, Kate responded: "Bring her up!"

Kate grew to enjoy Molly's company as much as Mom did, and later, if Kate learned that Molly was downstairs, she'd invite her up for dinner.

Dinner with
Michael Jackson

Kate's fan base was extensive and multigenerational, so it was no surprise when Michael Jackson reached out to her. In 1984, when the King of Pop was at the pinnacle of his career, he sought an invitation through Jane Fonda to dine at Kate's home. He called to set it up himself, saying he was a big fan of Spencer Tracy's.

One day, prior to the opening of the *Victory* concert tour, Kate looked up from the newspaper she was reading and called to Norah.

"Norah, I'm thinking of having Michael Jackson over for dinner. What do you think?" Norah was a Jackson fan by virtue of her kids' being crazy about him, yet she was also used to the star-studded cast that regularly descended upon Kate's home. She calmly continued her dusting before she responded. "Well, Ms. Hepburn," she said in her smooth and reassuring manner, "maybe you want to think about it for a night." Kate nodded, adjusted her reading glasses, and went back to her paper.

That evening Norah arrived home and, after catching up with the day's events, nonchalantly said, "Guess who might be coming to 244 East Forty-ninth for dinner?" By this time we were used to Mom's stories about people ranging from Christopher Reeve to Lauren Bacall, but she caught us all off guard with the news about Michael Jackson. I think we actually shrieked.

The next day, when Kate brought the subject up again, Norah announced that her kids had been thrilled with the news of this potential dinner guest. "Okay, then," Kate said. "Let's do it, dammit!"

Norah had heard that Michael Jackson didn't eat beef, one of Kate's favorites, but did enjoy a lot of vegetables, a favorite of Kate's as well. My mom also knew that Evian was his drink of choice. Norah prepared the Michael-influenced menu—seven vegetables as opposed to the usual five—as dictated by Kate.

Michael Jackson's autograph for my sister.

Dinner was a success. Michael was a bit shy and reserved, yet he was quite gracious—he was chatty with Kate and engaged in conversation with all of her guests. Michael was fascinated by his hostess and was especially interested in learning more about Spencer Tracy. Kate was riveted by the pop star's talent and skyrocketing career. The mutual admiration led to further dinner parties, as well as Michael's invitation for Kate, along with her good friend Laura Harding, Phyllis, and my mom, to be his guest at one of his concerts at Madison Square Garden.

On the night of the concert, Kate and company were whisked to the Garden in a white stretch limo. Led through a private access tunnel to the backstage, they were each introduced to Michael's parents and siblings. Each was presented with a set of earplugs, as well as her own personal bodyguard! Kate was dazzled by the entire experience—sparked by the energy and excitement of the crowd.

When the lights dimmed and the show began, Norah couldn't believe that the shy teenagelike man she had served dinner was commanding power and attention on stage with his attitude and incredible dance moves. Even thought they were enthralled with Michael's magic, the women found the music close to deafening, so when Kate gave Norah the "Let's go" nod after only two songs, Norah didn't protest.

Despite their early exit, Kate raved about the show for days and days.

Driving to Boca

All those who remained in Kate's employ had to be like the great actress in one respect: they had to be flexible. Katharine Hepburn did not want to hear that someone couldn't or wouldn't do a particular task.

If flexibility was the primary criterion for employment, then Howard Frederick Hildenbrand was certainly an ideal employee. The man known to us as Hilly was one of Mom's and my favorite characters to pass through 244. Though he worked for Kate for only four years, his vitality and sense of humor brought us all much joy. Hilly was the chauffeur, the waiter, and the man who would do whatever was needed at the moment it was needed.

But even the adaptable Hilly occasionally reached the end of his rope with his boss. This usually happened when Kate would have him make the long drive to Florida, where she enjoyed vacationing in Boca Grande. Kate used to remark that Florida was the jumping-off point to the next world—the churches are all packed because everyone is getting ready for the big trip! When he got back to New York, Hilly wasted no time telling Mom and me about his trip.

"Five hours into the ride, Norah, and I was ready to shoot myself! You have no idea what Kate is like in a vehicle." Of course Mom *did* know, but she loved to hear Hilly's yarns.

"So there we are: Kate's in front with me. Phyllis—bless her heart—is quietly sitting in the back, not saying a word, just nodding along," Hilly continued, shaking his head and laughing as he told his story.

"Of course you know Kate just can't be a passive passenger; she has to play driver. She must have told me twenty times, 'Hilly, move to your left now!' or 'Speed up, Hilly!'"

Hilly, like the rest of us, replied with a "Yes, Ms. Hepburn."

Hilly went on, "And then, *finally*, I get up enough nerve to turn on the radio." Being a bit dramatic, the chauffeur gestured in a kind of reenactment of the incident. "You should have seen the look on her face! She

Norah, Hilly, and me.

listened for a moment as if she didn't quite trust it or get it. And then she made her pronouncement, 'No! No! Turn that *off*, Hilly! It's too distracting!' Can you believe it? Telling me how to drive isn't—but the radio is!

"But you know, ladies, I can still make the ol' gal laugh!" Hilly would say, introducing us to his next tale. "Like the time she didn't have you, dear Norah, to serve her breakfast. The task was left, as you know, to yours truly. So there's Kate at the breakfast table with the tray of breakfast I had so expertly prepared when all of a sudden she starts yelling, 'Where's my honey? Where's my *honey*?' Upon hearing this, I realized I had forgotten to put honey on the tray for her Thomas's protein toast, and you know how much she loves that stuff." At this point Hilly stood up to re-create the moment. "So I come flying in the room—like this," he ran in out of breath, arms outstretched and reaching toward Mom, "and—now imagine you're Kate—I say, 'Here I am.'" He virtually flew onto one knee and landed next to Mom. "Kate looks at me, starts laughing hysterically, motions for me to produce the honey, which I held behind my back, and says, 'Aw, Hilly, you're hopeless.'"

At this point we would all be in stitches. Hilly would usually follow that story with a plea. "So please don't tell me Kate wants to go to Florida again," he'd say, looking desperately at my mom. "Three days with those two gals in the car will just about finish me off!"

Hilly's Chicken Piccata

Hilly introduced this recipe to Kate's kitchen. It was loved by all and was quickly integrated into Mom's dinner menus.

•　　•　　•

MAKES 2 TO
4 SERVINGS

½ cup grated Parmesan cheese
½ cup unbleached all-purpose flour
2 pinches of Italian seasoning
2 pinches of garlic powder
Pinch of pepper
2 eggs
¼ cup milk
4 chicken breast halves, boned and skinned
⅓ stick butter (or more as needed)
½ lemon

Combine the cheese, flour, Italian seasoning, garlic powder, and pepper in a paper bag and shake until blended. Transfer the mixture to a medium bowl and set aside.

In another medium bowl, whisk together the eggs and milk. Dip the chicken breasts in the egg mixture and then in the flour mixture, making sure they're well coated on both sides.

In a large frying pan, melt the butter. When the butter is foaming, add the chicken and fry the pieces until they are nicely golden on one side, about 10 minutes. Turn over the chicken breasts and fry for an additional 10 minutes, adding butter as needed. When the chicken is cooked through, transfer it to a serving platter, add a little fresh-squeezed lemon juice to each piece, and serve immediately or keep in a warm oven for a few minutes prior to serving.

Mom's Wedding Brooch

After Dad died, Mom had a rough time of it. With five kids and a full-time job, she was often exhausted and stressed. Then she met Jack. Jack Moore was a man who shared—and still shares—Mom's love of life, family, and all that relates to her native Ireland. Jack brought back a spark in Mom that had somehow faded over the years. Just a short time after they started dating, Mom's eyes began twinkling again, we recognized this as a reflection of the love she felt for this man. Kate saw it, too.

So it was no surprise when the couple announced they were to be wed. Based on the size of her family, Mom decided that eloping would be the best way to go. With so many kids, nieces and nephews, cousins, and aunts and uncles—not to mention friends—she just couldn't imagine dealing with an invitation list; a quiet affair seemed much more practical. Norah told Kate her plans, and though she was nervous about losing my mom to her new husband, Kate respected her desire for a no-fuss wedding. She approved of both Jack and the wedding plans.

Before Mom left to be married, Kate wanted to get her a gift. The actress recruited her dear friend Cynthia McFadden to help. They went to check out S. J. Shrubsole's classically elegant jewelry; Kate chose a stunning handmade English 18-karat-gold brooch, which featured a ruby-eyed American eagle holding a diamond.

"Norah dear," she called to Mom on the day before she was to elope with her fiancé, "I've got something I want you to have."

Kate presented Mom with the little jewelry box. Norah was delighted by its contents. "Oh, Ms. Hepburn," she said, overcome with emotion, as she pinned it on herself. "This is just so lovely." She touched it gently as she looked at her reflection.

Kate stood behind her, smiling. "Norah," Kate whispered. Their eyes locked in the hallway mirror. "I hope you won't leave me."

Mom didn't leave Kate. It was more like a new person was included in the 244 circle. And Jack was a welcome and wonderful addition.

Two Generations of Courage

On many occasions, Mom and my stepfather, Jack Moore, were invited to Kate's events, giving Mom the chance to flaunt the beautiful brooch Kate had given her as a wedding gift. One such event was the Planned Parenthood tribute in 1986, at which Ms. Hepburn was an honored guest. That evening the organization was also honoring Kate's mother, Katharine Martha Houghton, who was a pioneer in the establishment of Planned Parenthood. Kate's mother had died in 1951. Norah was proud to be attending; she was not only happy to have the opportunity to see her boss speak in public, she was also thrilled to have her new husband on her arm.

Kate had spent a considerable amount of time preparing for the evening. Earlier in the month, in Florida, she had been clocking hours in the Boca Grande Library (with the help of Hilly) doing research. She spent a long time writing her speech out on yellow lined paper.

Now the night had come, and Kate, along with her friend Laura Fratti, the pianist who taught her how to fake playing the piano for *West Side Waltz*, awaited the arrival of Mom and my stepfather. Jack wore a tuxedo borrowed from the actor Rod Colbin, who was also Kate's masseur, for the

Kate's mother, Katharine Martha Houghton.

evening. Norah was dressed in a simply designed, flattering black dress; the wedding brooch Kate had given her was placed delicately near the neckline. When Jack and Norah approached Kate to escort her to the Waldorf-Astoria for the evening's event, Kate let out an audible sigh. Laura was the first to speak. "Norah," she gasped, "you're gorgeous!" Kate smiled at Mom and added, "Absolutely!"

Kate and Laura were first out of the limousine that evening. Onlookers—stopped short by the scene of the forever-elegant grande dame making her entrance—watched in awe. Jack and Mom waited in the wake for the guest of honor and her friend to enter the hotel. As the handsome couple entered, Mom couldn't help but tenderly squeeze her husband's arm and whisper words from the old Irish song they often sang together: "It's a long way from Clare to here."

The evening featured a star-studded cast: the charismatic Walter Cronkite was the master of ceremonies, Barbara Walters and Martina Navrátilová were speakers at the dinner, and Angela Lansbury was teleconferenced in on a large screen. All extolled the virtues of planning a family, a cause the Hepburn family wholeheartedly supported. The highlight of the evening was Kate's speech. She had her yellow pages in front of her, and she referred to them from time to time, but the words clearly came from her heart. The crowd, which knew of both her reluctance to speak in public and her devotion to this cause, was appreciative, and they gave her a passionate standing ovation.

Robert Wagner

*I*n the 1980s, Robert Wagner was hot stuff. He received numerous Golden Globe nominations for his role in the TV drama *Hart to Hart*, not to mention the recognition he earned from his prolific movie and television roles. I don't know who was more smitten with him my mother or me. In any case, he proved to be a worthy target of our affection on the night of the tribute to Spencer Tracy in 1986, which the dashing Wagner hosted. Suave and unpretentious, the actor thrilled Kate with his performance.

Earlier that evening, in an Academy-sponsored tribute built around the premiere of the ninety-minute documentary *The Spencer Tracy Legacy: A Tribute by Katharine Hepburn*, sixteen hundred people had packed Broadway's Majestic Theatre. Frank Sinatra, Sidney Poitier, Robert Wagner, and director Stanley Kramer all spoke with great reverence about Tracy, a man some regard as the greatest movie actor of all time.

After the tribute, Kate hosted a large party in her 244 East Forty-ninth Street apartment. My mom organized us all: Hilly bartended and I served. Mom worked tirelessly to prepare, as instructed, several of Kate's favorite appetizers: shrimp cocktail, deviled eggs, prosciutto with melon, savory cheese snacks we called cheesies, and platters of fresh fruit and cheese. Of course Mom had also made her famous brownies and lace cookies. A full bar was offered, courtesy of Hilly's handiwork with the shakers, along with champagne.

Guests started flowing in. Robert Wagner arrived with Jill St. John and Claire Trevor. Cynthia McFadden and Susie Tracy, Spencer's daughter, followed, then Sidney Poitier, Kate's, Spencer's, and Katharine Houghton's *Guess Who's Coming to Dinner* costar.

While Mom was busy pulling and pushing things out of and into the oven, I walked around the crowded rooms and served the guests, who devoured Mom's treats as they listened to Kate's stories. Every room was buzzing with conversation that ranged from tales of Spencer's legacy to talk of current and future stars. Upon my return to the kitchen to refill my silver platter, I recognized the rich voice of Robert Wagner as he addressed my mom from the doorway.

"Now, who is responsible for all that wonderful food upstairs?" he asked, hesitating before stepping into Mom's territory. Mom, delighted, turned her back on the baking sheet of hot cheesies she had just removed from the oven, looked toward the actor, and grinned.

"Ah, those are kind words, Mr. Wagner." Mom blushed lightly. She wiped her hands and greeted him with a handshake that turned into a hug. I stepped in and she introduced me. "This is my daughter Eileen."

Though we were used to meeting—and serving—famous folks at 244, I felt my cheeks go warm as I shook Robert Wagner's hand. I had always admired the actor on television, but up close I was struck by how handsome he actually was! After shaking his hand, I stepped around him to fill my tray with hot cheesies.

Mom, however, had another job for me. "Mr. Wagner," she started, as he plucked one of the cheesies off the tray, "I was wondering if I could ask you a favor." Though his mouth was full, he smiled for Mom to continue. "Well," she started, "I was hoping we could take a picture—" He cut her off with "Of course!" and Mom shoved the camera into my hand.

Mr. Wagner wiped his hands before he reached for Mom. He smiled at me and said, "Whenever you're ready, Eileen." And though I was ready, I hesitated for a moment so that Mom's thrill could last a few seconds longer.

Robert Wagner hugging Mom.

Sidney Poitier

There were several goodies that Kate repeatedly asked my mom to prepare, and the lace cookies Norah made for the Spencer Tracy gala were certainly in the top five. These cookies were not only beloved by Kate, they also became quick favorites of her visitors to 244 East Forty-ninth Street. Sidney Poitier was one of many fans of Norah's lace cookies.

The evening of Kate's party for Spencer, Sidney, dashing and gracious, worked his way through the crowd and queued up along with the others to speak with Kate, greeting other guests as he waited. Finally he reached his former costar. Though I couldn't hear what he said, I knew he was talking about Spencer and the old days. He spoke with Kate for a bit, then gently brought the back of her hand to his lips and softly kissed it. He then headed toward the front door to leave the party.

Something stopped him, though—he caught sight of a platter of lace cookies. Mr. Poitier took two, smiled his thanks, and headed out the door.

A few seconds later, the doorbell rang. I looked out and to my surprise there was Mr. Poitier again. Assuming he had forgotten something upstairs, I opened the door, expecting him to rush by me. He stopped and looked at me with his gorgeous eyes. He wanted more cookies! I called to my mom, who immediately prepared a package of lace cookies for him. Delighted with his goody bag, Mr. Poitier gave my mom a big hug and headed out the door.

My mom, beaming, turned to me on the verge of a swoon. "What a hunk!" she pronounced as she headed back to the other guests.

Norah's Lace Cookies

• • •

MAKES ABOUT
3 DOZEN
COOKIES

⅛ pound butter (½ stick), softened
⅓ cup light brown sugar
½ cup turbinado sugar
1 egg, beaten
½ teaspoon vanilla
1 heaping teaspoon flour
1 cup chopped walnuts

Preheat the oven to 350° F. With a wooden spoon, mix the butter and sugar together, blending them until they are very soft. Add the egg and vanilla. Stir in the flour. Add the walnuts. Drop the batter by spoonfuls onto a cookie sheet covered with aluminum foil. Bake for 7 to 8 minutes. Let cool—sometimes Norah would stick trays in the freezer to hasten the cooling process but only for a couple of minutes—before removing and serving.

My Boyfriend

Kate was Mom's boss and on many occasions my boss. But she was also genuinely concerned about my well-being and happiness, not unlike a close relative.

One evening when I was in Manhattan, I traveled across town to meet my mother to go to a show. Luckily for us, Mom and I were frequently able to reap the benefits of Kate's theater connections. Kate often got us tickets for shows, and they were always house seats, in the first few rows. Running a bit behind—we were trying to grab a bite before curtain time—I stopped just for a moment to light a cigarette, then hastened my step. I assumed that Kate had already headed to Fenwick for the weekend, as usual, but as I walked down Forty-ninth Street, I noticed that her car was still there. Her chauffeur, Hilly, looked up and greeted me with a wave and a smile. I nonchalantly let the cigarette drop from my fingers, thinking that even with the evidence gone, I probably reeked of smoke. I also knew that if Hilly was there, Kate wasn't far behind.

Smoking was not something Kate condoned, though she had smoked years earlier and quit. I think the only one who ever smoked at 244 was

Sonny Mehta, her publisher at Knopf, and that was only because Kate didn't catch him in the act! So there I was, walking toward the car and imagining the lecture I would get; I could feel it in my stomach.

"Ms. Hepburn's in the car," Hilly announced as I moved closer. He opened the door for me and gave me a welcome pat on the back. Kate was sitting in the front seat.

I slunk into the driver's seat, trying to control my breath as I leaned over to receive her kiss. Kate took my hand and started asking me questions. I hadn't seen her for a couple of months and she wanted to catch up. She listened attentively as I told her about school and everything else that was going on in my life, including the guy I was dating. My stomach started to relax as I realized that I wasn't going to receive the verbal lashing I had anticipated. We concluded our discussion and kissed good-bye. I promised to come by again soon.

The following Monday, Kate mentioned to Mom that she had seen me and that I had sounded great. Kate wanted to know more about the boyfriend. Mom launched into her worries about my current steady. "He's a bit of a wild card," she confided. "The guy's a college dropout and I think that she's already spent too much time with him. Besides, if they were to get married, I'd never feel comfortable in his home!"

As usual, Kate took in what Norah had said before making her pronouncement. "Easy there," she said, patting Mom on the hand to calm her down. "Listen, Norah, you've got to tell Eileen that she's going nowhere with him." Mom was all ears as her boss continued. "Now, she probably won't listen, but you tell her I said, 'When the horse is dead, it's time to get off.'"

I did take Kate's advice but on my own schedule. Funny how your parents can say something, but when another adult—one whom you admire and whose opinion you greatly respect—says virtually the same thing, you consider it differently.

Kate's advice about so many things still rings in my head.

In the Garden with Kate

Mom and Kate's intense relationship was hard for outsiders to understand. The dynamics were of course dictated by the fact that the women were employer and employee. But still, Norah was always Norah, and Kate was always Kate. The two made quite a pair— they were very different, but they were both tenacious, tough yet tender women.

Mom had always been enamored of the excitement and independence New York City offered her. She says that New York City is her kind of place because it's vibrant day and night. In New York she can catch a bus—she doesn't drive—get a bite to eat, and come upon someone or something interesting. Norah is the kind of person whom people open up to. Whether it is on a park bench, in the market, or during a walk around town, Norah will glean some kind of information about the locals. On the other hand, I could live in a place for five years and still not know as much as my mom can find out in a day!

Because of her fame, Kate didn't have the luxury of being able to do things that Norah could. Instead of being able to talk freely with whomever she pleased, she was constantly approached by people who dreamed of a moment of conversation with the superstar. Kate sometimes seemed to envy Norah's freedom to chat with strangers. Kate also used to say, "You can't have it all!"

As different as they were, Kate was aware of how much Mom gave to others. Kate often said to Norah, "You work so hard, your children will do well and theirs will squander it! You know what they say, 'From shirtsleeves to shirtsleeves.' So take care of *you*! You've helped so many, but they're busy with their own lives."

Kate always worried about Mom. She was tough with her, too.

One day, they were in the garden arranging flowers, something they both enjoyed doing. They were chatting away when all of a sudden, Mom sensed that she was falling backward. Norah felt the pavement go out beneath her feet. Apparently the basement grate she was standing on had given way. Thankfully, her fall was broken by a small bar that she was able to grab hold of as she fell into the hole. Lying over the opening, firmly grasping the savior bar, she was stunned. Her back was on fire yet she tried to pull herself up. Just as she started to struggle her way out of the hole, the shadowy figure of her boss appeared above her. "Ms. Hepburn," Mom began, "I think I've hurt myself."

Kate's outstretched arm lengthened toward her employee. "Norah, get up!" Kate demanded as she hoisted Mom to her feet. "We've got guests for dinner!"

Mom limped out of the hole and brushed herself off, hurting terribly. But she quickly recovered her poise, and the two went back to finishing the floral arrangement. Though Mom was in pain, both women held fast to their credo of finishing tasks without whining.

Later that night, once the guests had gone, Mom quietly left the house, hoping some rest would ease the aches she had increasingly begun to feel as the hours passed. Two days later, she showed Kate her back. Kate had apparently forgotten all about it and was so surprised by the horrible bruises that she wanted to bring Mom immediately to the hospital for

Kate with her staff.

X-rays. But by then Mom figured she was fine; she just wanted Kate to know that she really had hurt herself.

When Norah told her sister Lillian about the incident, she said, "Good thing Kate has you! Most people would sue their employer over that kind of thing!" But Mom being Mom, she just shrugged the comment right off.

Liz Smith

Mom first met the columnist and author Liz Smith when Liz and Iris Love, the famous archeologist and socialite, were traveling home from Florida. Apparently Kate and Cynthia McFadden were on the same flight. They all had a lovely chat on the plane, and Kate subsequently reported to Norah, "Liz is a wonderful conversationalist, very well read, and a true Texan!" Since Kate had a Lincoln town car waiting outside at the airport, she offered the women a lift. Before dropping off her new friends, Kate invited them for dinner the following Monday evening.

Though Mom had no tolerance for what we kids liked or didn't like—she was of the you-eat-what-you're-served school—she had great interest in Kate's guests' preferences and wanted to accommodate them. Monday was fish night at 244 East Forty-ninth Street; when Norah learned that Liz didn't eat salmon, she decided to make a tasty bacon-wrapped shad roe. This was a great hit.

From the moment Liz and Iris arrived that evening with gorgeous bouquets to the time they left, the brownstone was alive with spirited conversation and laughter. Phyllis, Kate's secretary, asked Norah her impression of

Liz. Norah didn't hesitate in her response. "She's bright and she's funny. Let's have her back again!" She added, "Besides, she cleaned her plate!"

That was the first of many dinners Liz had at 244. And usually after those visits Kate would receive a copy of Liz's *New York Post* column in which she recounted highlights or references to the grande dame, along with a sweet thank-you card.

After Kate's death, Mom and Liz kept in touch. Liz has taken Mom out to lunch and invited her to spend the weekend in her Connecticut home. It was Liz who suggested that I put all our Kate tales and memorabilia together in this collection, and I am grateful to her.

Dearest Nora,

Mr. Sondheim and I send you our undying love and admiration. It was so great to see you recently at Miss Hepburn's. You looked great. You make such a difference wherever you go. Love to you.

Liz Smith

Liz

LIZ SMITH

NEWSDAY, MONDAY, APRIL 15, 1996

That Jaunty Kate!

'**I** WELCOME death! In death there are no interviews!" said Katharine Hepburn.

* * *

MISS HEPBURN might well have repeated this quote of hers more recently. Three weeks ago, the tabloids had her at death's door, and the supermarket tabs quoted her spouting nonsense about "going gently" and joining Spencer Tracy.

But one New York column reported last week that the great star was well on her way to recovery and had returned from Connecticut to her longtime NYC domicile — the Turtle Bay townhouse on East 49th, where neighbors supposedly observed her coming and going.

Part of this was correct. Miss Hepburn IS much improved since her recent illness. But let me assure you that the Great Kate hasn't set foot in Manhattan since she was felled by intestinal flu and had to be hospitalized.

When she left the hospital in mid-March, Kate went directly to her longtime family house on the edge of the Fenwick, Conn., golf course where she and other Hepburns have lived merrily for years, with the waters of Long Island Sound lapping their doorstep. It is here that Kate has plunged into icy waves for a daily swim, no matter the month.

* * *

I KNOW all this because I spent some of Easter weekend with Katharine Hepburn, and had a chance to observe her closely. She was quite perky, all dressed up in a tan cashmere turtleneck sweater, tan trousers and white running shoes. A Navy-blue sweater was tossed jauntily over her shoulders and her now-white hair was neatly caught back in a barrette. She was the picture of style, copied by everyone from Calvin Klein to The Gap.

Depending on the massive arm of her "main man," bodyguard and chauffeur, John Elmore, she came into her Fenwick living room to check that the fire was burning correctly. "Put another log on that," she ordered in her usual brisk fashion. Then she sat and examined cards and letters that continue to pour in from fans and pals. The masses of flowers were arranged and rearranged until she was satisfied, with the yellow blossoms she likes least weeded out. At one point, a bouquet of lilies arrived. Kate said, "That looks like something Howard Hughes would have sent!"

Asked about Hughes, she commented that his early serious deafness had been much neglected as a symptom of his behavior — a defining part of what made him tick and, perhaps, fall apart.

* * *

SHE HAS received, variously, in Fenwick — her sister, Peg; her brothers, Bob and Dick; her legion of nieces and nephews; the talented Kathy

Houghton, the niece who played her daughter in "Guess Who's Coming To Dinner?"; her writer friend from Hollywood, Scott Berg; her lawyer, Erik Hanson; her NYC housekeeper, Nora Moore; her director pal, Anthony Harvey. Lauren Bacall rang up to chat.

* * *

ASKED IF she missed being in the city, Kate said: "No, I don't miss New York. Indicating Fenwick, she asked, "Aren't I lucky to be able to have this and be here?" She expressed interest in getting into the golf cart left to her by the late George Cukor to make a tour of

Katharine Hepburn
At home and happy

Film Photo

Fenwick. "That will be *thrilling!*" she said somewhat sarcastically.

Told that she had been all but buried by the tabloids, she was incredulous. "I never made any of those statements to anyone. I certainly didn't say anything about 'joining Spencer.' Such rubbish!"

The star ate at least two trencherman meals prepared by her Fenwick cook, Hong Luong. One menu featured steak, potatoes, green beans, fruit salad and cauliflower au gratin. Another meal consisted of ham, green beans, potatoes, bread, macaroni and cheese, and hot cross buns. After finishing off both these meals, she asked for coffee ice cream.

* * *

KATHARINE HEPBURN is *the* great legend of American films and the State of Connecticut, and anywhere else she happens to hang her hat. She will be 89 years old in May and seems to be going strong.

When I pointed out that there was a story in the new Howard Hughes biography that has a young Kate standing on a ledge, threatening to commit suicide over her love for Howard, someone close to her laughed: "Suicide!? Well, I can imagine Kate committing homicide — but suicide? Never!!"

Dinner for a Crowd

Mom usually had some notice before company came, but there were many occasions on which Kate—who obviously had faith in Mom's ability to magically bring together meals for many folks—would call just hours before a crowd was about to descend. That was what happened the day of the funeral service for one of Kate's friends, the director and actor Noel Willman.

Kate was in a bit of a tizzy; Noel was very important to her. They had met when he directed her in the Broadway production of *A Matter of Gravity* in 1976. After that he became a frequent dinner guest up until the time of his death in 1988. On the spur of the moment, Kate decided that it would be nice to invite the funeral guests back to 244 for a supper gathering. That left Mom only three hours to pull together a meal for twenty-five guests!

Mom immediately flew into action. She took stock of the pantry and the fridge and found it full of vegetables. She knew she had some stewing beef as well. Aha, she thought, beef stew it is! As she began to prepare it, she felt a surge of panic and thought that pulling it all together in time

185

might be tough. Ms. Hepburn expected flawlessness, and that weighed heavily on Mom. But then something wonderful happened—there was a knock on the kitchen door. To Norah's surprise and relief she saw her sister Lillian, along with three friends who were in town sightseeing. Norah was sure that God had intervened. Without missing a beat, Mom welcomed them in. "You're just in time, ladies! I've got a task for all of you!"

Lillian and her friends were as adept in the kitchen as Mom, so the four women got to work cutting vegetables and setting up the house. Norah sent Lillian over to her friend Louis's to borrow needed supplies.

Things were moving along nicely when the phone rang; Ms. Hepburn was on the line. "Norah, Noel loved you, too! You should be here. Now get over here!" Norah's sister and friends understood Kate's request, and, after being left very clear instructions, they shooed the head chef out the door.

When the service for Noel Willman concluded, Kate stayed behind to chat with friends and to help escort them to her home. Norah scurried out and back to her kitchen, where she found everything all set for the guests' impending arrival. She thanked her "staff" for their herculean efforts and cleared them from the house moments before the guests arrived.

The meal, served buffet style, went off without a hitch. Kate and her guests, which included Zoë Caldwell and Robert Whitehead, ate the stew in little bowls, together with a gorgeous mixed green salad. The meal ended with Norah's irresistible treats: freshly baked brownies and cookies.

Norah's Beef Stew

• • •

SERVES 6 TO 8

⅔ cup all-purpose flour
1½ pounds stewing beef, cut into 1-inch cubes
3 teaspoons olive oil
2½ cups beef bouillon
Salt and pepper to taste
Bay leaf, if desired
1 cup pearl onions, or 2 medium onions, finely chopped
1 package carrots, peeled and diced into ¼-inch pieces
1 cup chopped mushrooms
6 to 8 small red potatoes, peeled and cut in half
1 cup peas

Put the flour into a large mixing bowl or onto a wooden cutting board. Evenly coat each piece of beef. In a medium saucepan, heat the oil. Lower the flame and brown the meat for 5 to 7 minutes. Add oil as needed. Drain the meat on paper towels.

In a large saucepan with a lid, combine the meat and beef bouillon. Bring to a boil, then lower the heat and cover. Simmer for about 2 hours, or until the meat is nearly tender. Add salt and pepper to taste and the bay leaf, if using. Add the onions, carrots, mushrooms, and potatoes and cook for 35 minutes. Add the peas and cook for 10 more minutes. Serve immediately.

Garson Kanin's Betrayal

So many people were a part of Kate's life—and therefore our lives—during Mom's thirty-year tenure with the Hollywood icon. If we didn't actually meet someone, my Mom, the consummate raconteur, was able to bring the person to life in her stories.

Garson Kanin came into Kate's life early on; along with the famous actress Ruth Gordon, his wife, he wrote the fabulous Hepburn-Tracy comedies *Adam's Rib* and *Pat and Mike*. Though he wrote and directed many plays, he was best known for many years in my home as the man who betrayed Kate and Spencer.

Mom always respected people's privacy; she felt that there were certain things that others didn't need to know. Kanin's book went against her philosophy. *Tracy and Hepburn: An Intimate Memoir* was published in 1971 and immediately became a best seller. It revealed aspects of Ms. Hepburn's private life that she considered highly personal. Kate, who did not typically hold grudges, was horrified when she learned that Kanin had committed the ultimate betrayal; because he was so specific in his storytelling, Kate often said that he could have only been able to document a lot of the text by wearing a hidden microphone when he came to dinner at her house.

After the book was published, Garson and his wife were exiled from Kate's life. Kate often told my mom and others that he would have never had the guts to publish the book while Spencer was alive. She said Spencer would have killed him.

Kate was someone who couldn't stay angry forever, though she did keep Kanin away for more than twenty years. In the early nineties, Kate decided to forgive his disloyalty and phoned him to invite him over for dinner. Because Kate was very concerned about how the evening might unfold, she insisted that her friend Cynthia McFadden also be present. Kanin accepted the invitation and brought along his new wife, Marian Seldes.

Over the course of the dinner, Kate and her guests realized that they had too much to share with one another, and so the past betrayal was forgotten. Afterward, Kate and Kanin sat together, immersed in old stories as if they were the only two people in the room. Later that evening, after Kanin had left, Kate remarked to Cynthia a powerful insight that she had gleaned: "After more than twenty years of not speaking with each other, tonight I recognized that I missed him more than he missed me." Perhaps the feeling was more mutual than Kate realized, for that was the first of several dinners they shared, and Kanin always brought flowers or something special for his old friend.

Garson Kanin was not an easy guest. He was a bit gruff and set in his ways, especially about his likes and dislikes in terms of the food he was served, but Mom didn't mind him. Phyllis, Kate's secretary, always liked him.

Later Kate gave Norah's husband, Jack, an autographed copy of Kanin's book. I guess she wanted us to read it after all.

Honor at the
Kennedy Center

*I*n 1990, on the morning of the day that Kate was to receive the Kennedy Center Honors for her lifetime contribution to the arts and American culture, Norah was, as usual, looking after her eighty-three-year-old boss.

"Ms. Hepburn," called Norah from the bedroom landing at 244 East Forty-ninth. "I just came upstairs to make sure you're all set for tonight."

Kate called back to Norah, "I'm almost ready. Come in."

My mom looked at Kate, who was putting the finishing touches on her bun. Though Norah had worked with Kate for close to twenty years at that point, she was still impressed by the star's presence.

"Receiving the Kennedy Center Honors is quite a compliment," Norah remarked proudly as she watched Kate get up and gather the rest of the items she'd be taking on her trip to Washington, D.C. Kate's schedule for the next couple of days included a gala at the White House, and though Kate was not one for a lot of pomp and circumstance, she knew she'd better get a bit fixed up for the occasion. Kate's elegant sophistication transcended what some considered the norms of fashion; she always had her own style. That's part of what my mom, and the rest of the world, loved about her.

"You think so?" Kate responded to my mother's comment about the Honors. "Well," she said, "I haven't got a jacket for this outfit. Really, Norah, I can't find anything!" Kate chuckled and started to reminisce.

"It's funny, Norah, but I can't help but think of what Spencer used to say to me," Kate started. "I always think about his words when I recall the robbery. Remember the break-in?" Norah had actually lived the story, but like my daughter, Grace, who'll ask me to tell the same bedtime tale again and again, Mom nodded for Kate to go on.

"You came in after the house was empty for the weekend and there in the center of the roof—right above us—was that gaping hole!" Kate spoke with as much emotion as she had when she told the story for the first time. "I still can't believe those crooks scaled the roof and then cut it open." Kate shook her head as she said, "Lucky for us it didn't rain. What a mess that would have been!"

Mom remembered the incident well; she had come to work that Monday morning in the early 1970s and was horrified to discover not only the intrusion but also that the thieves had landed in the space where Kate kept all her personal records dating back to 1931. They stole her heirloom silver, jewelry, and minks, ransacking the house from top to bottom. Most devastating to Kate beyond the invasion of privacy was the fact that they had taken things of great personal value.

"Those fools." Kate sighed. She saddened and looked distant for a moment. Then a smile started to dance across her face. "But Spencer's words have always put things in perspective for me! Oh, Spencer. How he loved to tease me! He never was much for all those furs and jewels, and whenever he came across them, he'd say 'Ah, Katie, where would you be going in your finery anyway?'"

She brushed my mom's hand as she stood up. Both women had withdrawn into the memories of loves who were no longer living. Kate

To Katharine Hepburn
with admiration and congratulations, *Katharine Hepburn* *me, Too.* *George Bush* *Barbara Bush*

suddenly eyed my mother's outfit with a quizzical look. "Norah dear, that's a nice coat. Can I borrow it?"

My mom instantly removed it. "Of course, Ms. Hepburn. But are you sure?"

"Quite," Kate pronounced as she tried it on. "Yes, this will do *very* nicely." Kate turned, admiring herself in the mirror.

"But first, Ms. Hepburn, I need to tell you something about it."

"What's that, Norah?" Kate asked, continuing to appreciate the coat. Kate's curiosity was piqued; she couldn't imagine what my mom was about to say.

"You should know, Ms. Hepburn, I got the coat years ago in a thrift shop," Mom confessed, a bit sheepishly.

At that Kate smiled grandly. "All the better then," she pronounced as she grabbed her bag and headed down to the car that was waiting to whisk her off.

Biographies and Autobiographies

*A*lmost immediately after Kate passed away, in 2003, Scott Berg's *Kate Remembered* came out. The day after she died, the news media announced the publisher's upcoming release; the book hit the stores twelve days later. For my mom as well as many of those in Kate's close circle, the timing was a surprise; they felt it was just too soon after Kate's death. They also complained about the way their beloved Kate was frequently portrayed in the book.

Years earlier, Scott had struck up a friendship with Irene Selznick, who introduced the young writer to her friend Kate. In the years that followed, Scott became a frequent dinner guest at the brownstone, traveling in from his home in California. He would stay at the house during the week as well as on weekends, when Kate was off at Fenwick, though sometimes Scott would take off with her to Fenwick, too.

Scott was not just any guest; he had earned house privileges at 244. It was a neat arrangement for a writer of biographies. In Kate's private residence, on the weekends when he had 244 to himself, he had unlimited access to all of the star's diaries, memorabilia, and her private files. But there was more to be found upstairs if one took the time to look. Years earlier, after Kate closed up the house she shared with Spencer in California, she had brought home with her the personal diaries of her beloved partner of close to three decades.

Norah got to know the famous biographer pretty well. He was certainly around a lot, and Kate liked and respected him. Mom was also impressed by him—even more so when he told her he had taken ten years to write *Goldwyn*, one of several of his highly acclaimed biographies. But it was something else that impressed her even more. Due to Kate's sheer generosity, Scott became a part of a privileged group of friends whom Kate honored by allowing them to use her home while she was away. Unlike many of Kate's other friends, though, Berg never brought the star chocolate or flowers.

A few weeks after *Kate Remembered* came out, Mom unexpectedly received a copy from Scott with a note saying he hoped it would bring back to her a few good memories of their dear friend. Everyone in and out of Kate's circle asked Mom what she thought of the book. Of course Norah was appreciative of Scott's hard work and his gift, but she was reserved in her commentary. She would say, "For the best read on Kate, march down to the local bookstore and pick up a copy of *Me*. Kate worked so hard on that—and that's the truth."

Lauren Bacall

When Katharine Hepburn gave me a copy of her book *The Making of the African Queen, or How I Went to Africa with Bogart, Bacall and Huston and Almost Lost My Mind,* I didn't think too much about it. I was immature and much more interested in things other than reading about the former escapades of my mom's boss. Mom, however, was acutely aware of the fact that the people I was meeting would shape my worldview.

Lauren Bacall was someone Mom had always admired for her grace, intelligence, and work ethic. Norah had the privilege of meeting Bacall, who was a frequent visitor to 244 East Forty-ninth Street. Kate and Lauren had met in 1951 when *The African Queen* was being shot; Betty (her birth name and the name she was affectionately called by Kate, Bogie, and many others) joined her husband and Kate during their adventuresome shooting of the movie. That was the beginning of a friendship that lasted over fifty years. Kate later became the godmother of Lauren Bacall's son, Sam.

Not long after the publication of Kate's book *Me*, Ms. Bacall came by for dinner. The two friends were busy discussing the book, and Lauren mentioned that she would love a copy for Sam. Kate was delighted. "I'd do anything for Sam," she said as she started to sign the book. She added, "But Betty, do tell me his wife's name." Apparently she was going to sign it to both of them.

Lauren waved her hand as she responded, "Oh, just Sam will do. I don't know if this will last!"

"To Sam then," Kate said without missing a beat.

There's another story Mom loves to tell about one of her favorite 244 visitors. Once when Kate had invited Lauren for dinner, Ms. Bacall was running a bit behind. Kate was upstairs waiting while Norah was down in the kitchen, putting the final touches on the meal. Suddenly the door flew open and Lauren came in—windswept but totally gorgeous and apologizing profusely. As she helped the beautiful actress remove her coat and set down her bags, Norah told her that Kate was still up in the living room and that dinner hadn't been served yet. As Mom hung up Lauren's coat, she said, "Ms. Bacall, there's something I've been wanting to ask you."

Lauren brushed a stray strand of hair out of her eyes before focusing all her attention on Mom. "Of course." Lauren encouraged Mom with a broad smile.

"Well, I was just wondering, . . . Well, why is it that you keep working and pushing yourself so hard? I mean at this stage of the game . . ."

Lauren smiled at Norah. At that point, Kate, who had apparently heard the activity downstairs, called down to inquire as to the whereabouts of her dining partner and her dinner.

"Be right there," Lauren answered. "Norah," she said to Mom as she turned toward her, "We are all working girls, aren't we? And who doesn't need the money?" With that, the elegant actress smiled and headed upstairs.

Anthony Quinn

Kate was never a fan of surprises. Not long after her arrival in Vancouver in 1993 to shoot the television movie *This Can't Be Love*, she learned that her costar Peter O'Toole had backed out at the last minute. Upon hearing this, she announced to Norah that she was ready to pack up her things and head back to New York. My mother, along with the producers, tried to calm Kate down. The frantic producers found their next leading man: Anthony Quinn. Of course Kate had the final say.

A dinner meeting between Mr. Quinn and Ms. Hepburn was arranged, to take place in Kate's Canadian penthouse apartment, rented for Kate during the shoot. Anthony arrived, introductions were made, and Norah asked what she could serve the six-foot-tall Mexican actor—and famous womanizer—whom she had seen on the screen ever since she was a young girl. My mom was devastated when Mr. Quinn requested vodka, which was not in the bar of their rented home. Norah headed back to the kitchen to double-check, knowing that Kate would be furious if she learned they weren't fully stocked—it was also a national holiday in Canada so the liquor stores were closed.

This Can't be Love

October 12 - November 10, 1993

Norah opted to serve Mr. Quinn a glass of water on the rocks. He graciously accepted it and even asked for another midway through the meal. Always the charmer, Mr. Quinn convinced Kate and everyone else that he should be the leading man. Kate was smiling again.

As Norah was cleaning up, Mr. Quinn stopped by the kitchen. A giant in voice and size, he wrapped one arm around my mother. Looking down at my mom with a smile and a wink, he pronounced, "And I must say, Norah, that was the best damn vodka I've ever had!"

(facing page) The cast and crew of *This Can't Be Love*.

Kate's Favorite Beet Soup

Homemade soup was one of the Hepburn kitchen mainstays, and it was served at every dinner. The actress not only enjoyed eating soup, she also relished touting its benefits and sharing her love of it with her friends. Kate's favorite, beet soup, was always served cold, no matter what time of year. Because her boss loved it so much, Norah made huge batches, then stored whatever she didn't serve in jars in the fridge. Kate would always scoop up a few to take with her to Fenwick. Mom kept plenty of containers on hand so that guests could take beet soup home to enjoy.

• • •

MAKES 8 TO
10 CUPS

4 large beets
1 small red onion, peeled and sliced
1 cucumber, seeded and coarsely chopped
1 cup chicken broth
One 33-ounce bottle Mother's borscht
1 cup sour cream or plain yogurt
Juice of 1 to 2 lemons, plus lemon zest for garnish
Salt and pepper to taste
¼ cup chopped fresh dill, for garnish

Gently wash the beets to get rid of the dirt. Be careful not to break the skin, or the beets will get mushy and lose flavor when you cook them. Place the beets in a medium saucepan and add cold water to cover. Bring to a boil, then reduce the heat, cover the pot, and simmer until the beets are tender, between 40 minutes and an hour depending on the size of the beets. Check for tenderness by picking up a beet and giving it a quick squeeze with your fingers. When the beets are tender, drain them and run them under cold water, then trim the tops and bottoms and remove the skin. Let the beets cool completely, then slice them and place them in the blender.

Add the onion, cucumber, and chicken broth and blend. Pour in the borscht and sour cream or yogurt. Add the lemon juice and salt and pepper. Purée until well blended.

Pour into soup bowls. Garnish with dill and lemon and serve.

Mom's Boss and
My Wedding

*I*t wasn't that I didn't want Katharine Hepburn at my wedding. After all, she was Mom's boss and she had been a very important part of my family's life for years prior to my big day. But it was *my* big day, and as the bride in a wedding of two very large families—with 320 invitees—I had so many details to take care of that making sure everything was okay for Kate seemed like just one more. Now, of course, the impatience I had then seems not only foolish but childish.

The logistics of getting Kate to my wedding required careful consideration. I was to be married to Thomas Joseph Meara on December 31, 1992, at Manhattan College in Riverdale, New York, where both my husband and I went to college. We were getting married on New Year's Eve, so we also had to think about the weather, not to mention the stairs—for even though Kate was in great shape, she was eighty-five years old. After much discussion, Hilly, the chaplain, and I surveyed the grounds and came up with an alternate route to the chapel so that Kate could bypass the many steps. The plan was for Kate to be dropped off on the road above and then slip in the chapel through the door closest to the altar.

With my husband, Tom Meara, on our wedding day.

Even with all the plans set, I was nervous. I remember calling my pal Maura and asking her whether she *really* thought it was a good idea for Kate to attend. Maura had heard me ask her the same question several times with increasingly heightened anxiety, and she consistently responded with the same levelheaded patience. Finally, after days of my whiny prodding, Maura grabbed me by the shoulders, looked me square in the eyes,

Phyllis and Kate at my wedding.

and said to me, "Hey, listen, Eileen. Let's just stop this nonsense! It's not like Cindy Crawford will be there. Who do you think you're competing with anyway? It's *your* wedding day!" Maura also reminded me that the crowd would expect Kate to be there because it was my mom's day, too.

Maura was half right. Of course she wasn't Cindy Crawford, but Kate was one of America's greatest icons.

In the end, Kate put us all in our places. She came right up all those steps we had arranged for her to avoid, and she entered through the main door, escorted by her niece Katharine Houghton. One look at my wedding video shows the stir she caused; you can see the entering guests elbowing each other, nodding, and whispering while furtively glancing in Kate's direction. Mom was beaming.

After the wedding ceremony, some of the guests were not so discreet, and they started swarming toward the famous actress, some just looking, some wanting desperately to be introduced. Decades of dealing with the public had given Kate plenty of experience in shirking flocks of folks. Poised as always, Kate rose with the help of her beautiful niece and walked toward me; she was first in the receiving line. She kissed me and held my left hand in both of hers. She leaned in and whispered, "You're a beautiful bride, Eileen." With a gentle squeeze of my hand, she was off.

It's funny how we often want to reach back and savor something wonderful—a moment we feel we didn't relish enough when it happened. When I'm reminded of that moment with Kate, I smile.

Warren Beatty

*W*arren Beatty's charm was instrumental in convincing Kate, at age eighty-six, to appear in the 1994 film *Love Affair*. Working on the film meant not only that she had to travel to California but also that she'd be gone for several weeks. Kate acquiesced but requested that home be brought with her. Home came in the form of my mom.

Warren, being Warren, never gave up an opportunity to try to dazzle the superstar he was so taken with. Kate may have been enchanted by Warren, but she always held her ground with him. My mom still loves to tell the story of their first step in the *Love Affair* adventure.

The Warner Brothers private jet was waiting on the tarmac for Mom and Kate when they arrived at the airport in New York. Kate was too busy with her let's-get-on-with-the-show attitude to be impressed by the cushiness of their carrier. Sensing Kate's impatience, Warren tried to provide some distraction.

"Ladies," he said as he sat deep into a chair you'd more likely find in a living room than on an airplane, "it won't be too long now." Kate fastened her seat belt and settled in, her script on her lap, looking over the rim of her reading glasses at Norah, who knew she was not comfortable sitting there in a small plane that wasn't moving. Warren must have sensed this as well.

He looked over at my mom conspiratorially and winked as he embarked on a distraction mission. "So, Kate," he began, "since we're waiting here for a while, would you like to hear about my love life?" Mom stifled giggles as she looked over at Warren, who was eagerly awaiting a response from Kate.

Kate lowered the script she was attempting to study. "*Really*, Warren," she said, "who *cares*?" She picked up the script and resumed reading. The unflappable Warren shrugged his shoulders but snuck another glance at my chuckling mother before moving on to his newspaper.

Prior to flying out to California to shoot *Love Affair*, Warren Beatty had secured a lovely house for Kate and Mom to stay in. His goal was to keep Ms. Hepburn happy—not always an easy task.

Though the house was certainly comfortable—it had the requisite fireplace, which was the primary amenity that Kate consistently demanded—things were not perfect. Despite all of Warren's efforts, including late-evening visits to check on the star, Kate still kept threatening to leave for New York on the next plane. My mom told us that during that period, Warren and Kate fell into the respective roles of dutiful son and demanding mother.

One evening, Warren had come by as usual to check on his favorite visitor. "I'll be back to see you tomorrow morning at nine-thirty," he pronounced as he blew Kate a kiss goodnight. She dismissed him with a wave and went back to the book she had been reading.

The next morning, at precisely nine o'clock, Kate was waiting. Norah was cleaning up and getting ready for the next meal, wondering if Warren knew that although Kate had heard Warren say nine thirty, she expected him to come before then. According to Ms. Hepburn, that's how one conducted oneself professionally; a nine thirty appointment signaled a nine o'clock arrival. Time was passing. Kate sat calmly in the living room, reading her paper, but Norah knew she was thinking, How could he make me wait like this?

As Norah dried her hands on a dish towel, she glanced at the clock, which now read nine thirty, then she caught sight of Warren jogging up the path. Norah sighed, bracing herself for what was about to come.

SENT BY:WB/STEVE SPIRA   :12-13-93 : 10:35 :   818 954 2487-212 268 9406   :# 6/ 9

VIA FAX   *Red-lined*

December 9, 1993
Revised December 13, 1993

Ms. Katharine Hepburn
10 Mohegan Avenue
Fenwick, Old Saybrook, Connecticut 06475

Re: "LOVE AFFAIR"

Dear Ms. Hepburn:

WB, Warren and everyone associated with "LOVE AFFAIR" are very excited that you have agreed to render acting services as "Ginny" in the picture. The following will confirm the agreed upon terms in connection with such services.

1.   **START DATE**

You travel to Los Angeles this weekend and start rehearsals on Monday, December 13th. Your services in connection with principal photography will begin either Wednesday, the 15th, Thursday the 16th, or Friday the 17th, depending on the length of rehearsals.

If there is a delay in your travel date to Los Angeles, these dates will be pushed back accordingly.

2.   **FEE; LENGTH OF SERVICES**

You will receive a guaranteed fee of   for required rehearsals, up to nine days plus two free days of principal photography and three free post-production days (the post-production days include, but are not limited to, looping, and need not be consecutive). The number of days of principal photography is greater than originally discussed to accommodate your request that you not work more than seven hours "before the cameras" on any one day. Hair, make-up and wardrobe time is not included in the seven hour limitation, and neither is the one hour lunch break you requested.

In the event your services are required in excess of the aggregate number of days set forth above, you will be entitled to overages at the rate of   per day. We have agreed that you will not be required to work more than five consecutive days without a day off.

"Warren's here, Ms. Hepburn," Mom announced as he approached the kitchen door.

He gave my mom one of his big hugs, thundered, "Where's my lovely lady?" and went to look for Kate.

Kate was already up. She had thrown down her paper and was heading toward the doorway. "It's about time, Warren. You're *late*!" she scolded.

Warren stepped back. "But Ms. Hepburn, it's just nine thirty!" he said, half laughing and half apologizing. Kate reached up and placed her hands on his shoulders. "Young man," she started. He looked serious now and was listening attentively. "If you want to be an actor and stay long in this business, remember to make sure you're ahead of those you want to impress." Warren nodded as he took in the advice. Kate continued, "Why, my own father would have driven away if we were ever a moment late!"

Norah knew that Kate didn't understand that Warren already had significant stature in the Hollywood community.

Warren apologized—of course. Mom says that after that, he was much more careful about his timing.

The Irish Repertory Theater

Katharine Hepburn put her money where her mouth was—if she believed in a cause, she supported it through action and deed.

Ciarán O'Reilly and Charlotte Moore, two friends of Katharine Houghton's, started the Irish Repertory Theater in the summer of 1987 with the intention of bringing Irish and Irish American works to the New York stage. Of course Mom was enamored of the whole mission of the theater group. In 1993, the Irish Repertory Theater approached Kate to ask if she'd introduce a production they were working on: a celebration of Yeats's work for a one-night-only benefit performance at the Booth Theatre in Manhattan. This event, which would feature Mia Farrow, Claire Bloom, and Milo O'Shea, among other well-known Irish and Irish American talents, was to be held just after Kate had surgery on her foot. Kate planned to be there and nothing was going to deter her.

That evening was a big one for Mom as well. Though she had attended several Irish Repertory Theater productions, she was thrilled to see Kate speak. My youngest brother, Bill, and my stepfather also joined the audience that evening.

Bill, who was a bit more peripherally involved in 244 life than my sister and me, remembers that evening quite well. Like all of us, Bill was often questioned about his Mom's famous boss. And like the rest of us, he held her in high esteem. But it wasn't until he saw her talk that he realized how extraordinary she was. That night, he remembers seeing Kate stride across the stage. She had left her cane backstage; she didn't want to be seen publicly with it. Proud, poised, and charismatic, she—as always—commanded everyone's attention. Bill noticed that Kate exuded a kind of electricity.

Mom was running a bit late that evening—getting Kate to the theater and backstage had taken longer than she anticipated—so she couldn't make it to her seat. Still, she got to hear Kate speak, and she stood in back by herself watching the production. Ciarán and Charlotte, who had saved a seat for Mom beside them, eventually found her and invited her to the after-party at Sardi's. Of course she would have loved to have gone, but by the time she got her boss home and tucked into her cozy bed after the big night, the gang would have already departed. She didn't mind too much, though. What mattered most to Mom was that the event had been a tremendous success, thanks in great part to the generosity of her boss.

An Invitation from Bob Dylan

Though Kate was a homebody who loved her hearth and home-cooked meals more than anything else, she received endless invitations to attend parties of all sorts, which she more often declined than accepted.

One day in the mid-1990s, a handsome, well-dressed man rang the bell at 244 East Forty-ninth Street. Norah opened the door and said, "Yes, sir. How can I help you?" He explained that he had come on behalf of his boss, Bob Dylan, who was currently living next door.

"Mr. Dylan," the man continued, "requested that I pass this note along to Ms. Hepburn." He handed the note to Norah. "Mr. Dylan's daughter is having a party this evening, and he would be delighted if

242 East 49th Street
New York 17, N.Y.

Dear KATharine HopBurn
  My daughter is having a graduating
Party in the rented house next door
to you, (the one with the dog)
it will be from 7:30 to 10 - if
you could stop by, you'd be most
welcome
                Bob Dylan

Ms. Hepburn could stop by." My mom must have had her I-don't-think-so look on, because he added, "You come, too, with Ms. Hepburn. Mr. Dylan would like that. It will be a nice party—you'll see."

"That's lovely," my mother said. "I'll see to it that Ms. Hepburn gets this." Norah graciously accepted the invitation. The gentleman thanked her and walked away. My mom passed the note along to Kate, who, as usual, chose to spend the evening at home.

Mom's Hot Toddy

This warm drink, Mom's cure-all, was served on several occasions to both Kate and her guests. Mom suggests that if you're not feeling well, just before going to bed take two aspirin and drink this tonic. The mixture not only sweats out an oncoming cold, it also encourages a good night's sleep.

•   •   •

SERVES 1

1½ shots whiskey
1 teaspoon honey
1 cup boiling water
½ teaspoon fresh-squeezed lemon juice

Pour the boiling water, whiskey, honey, and lemon juice into a large glass (with a spoon inside to prevent the glass from breaking). Stir well.

The President and Mrs. Clinton

request the pleasure of your company

at a reception to be held at

The White House

on Sunday, December 4, 1994

at five-thirty o'clock

Black Tie

Helping the Restaurant Workers

Kate was never one to ignore what was happening around her, so when workers at the Box Tree Restaurant, located just a few doors down on Forty-ninth Street, started striking in the late 1990s, she took notice. Mom got the scoop as she passed by the picketers and passed the word on to her inquisitive boss. The mostly Latino waiters and busboys, who alleged unfair labor practices by the posh French restaurant's new owner, welcomed their supportive neighbors.

On one occasion, Kate stopped to chat with the workers and inquire about how they were faring. The fall chill was in the air. Kate admired their tenacity but was concerned about the lowering temperatures. As she left them that evening, she threw up her fist and shouted "Don't quit!" in solidarity. Walking into her brownstone, she asked Mom to bring the group some sandwiches, cookies, and hot coffee, which Mom delivered with pleasure.

The strike wore on for years, and Norah, at Kate's request, continued to send out food from time to time. Kate also urged Norah to tell the men that they could come by if they needed to use the bathroom or get hot coffee.

More of a realist than an idealist, Mom was a bit reluctant; she worried about letting complete strangers into the house.

During the course of the multiyear strike, it was not unusual to find the ladies of 244 chatting with the group. At one point, the workers sent Norah and Kate a basket of flowers in gratitude for their steadfast support.

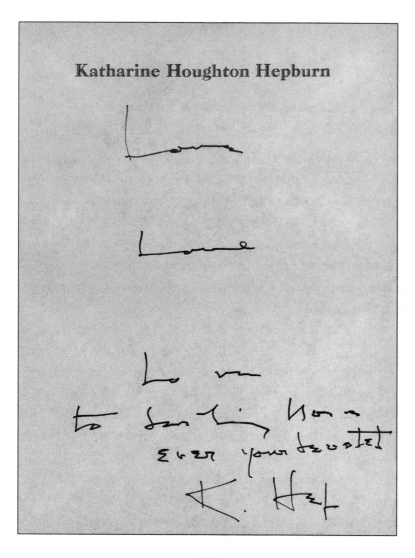

Caring for Kate

During the last few years with Kate, Mom needed more help; she was increasingly finding that she couldn't take care of the cooking, the house, and her beloved employer, who was now suffering from periods of disorientation and forgetfulness. This was a difficult time for all of us. Seeing Kate, who was so quick-witted all her life, frequently lose her bearings was heart wrenching. But there were still times when a glimmer of the Great Kate we knew and loved would come shining through.

When things got too tough for Mom to handle alone, she decided she had to hire someone to stay with Kate at night. Luckily, she didn't have to look too far to find a discreet and trustworthy person. My mom's first choice was her sister Lillian, my godmother.

Lillian was perfect for the job of caring for Kate. She had a great disposition; her cheeriness was genuine and contagious. She was also well qualified, having spent years caring for a wealthy woman in East Hampton.

As soon as Lillian took the job, Mom felt a huge sense of relief. Lillian would sit in the dark bedroom while Kate slept. Mom was worried that if she was in another room, she wouldn't get to Kate fast enough. (At that point, the newspapers—which Mom kept out of sight—said that Kate was on her deathbed.) Kate had good days and bad days; there were many factors affecting her decline. She had eye problems from her famous fall into the Venetian canal during the shooting of *Summertime,* she had had hip surgery in the 1970s and a terrible foot accident in the 1980s, and she suffered from skin cancer and now memory lapses as well.

One night, Norah stayed over and was sleeping on the couch in the living room, which was directly below Kate's bedroom, when she heard a noise. She was up with a start, glanced at the clock, which read 2:00 A.M., then heard a commotion coming from Kate's room. Grabbing a robe, she darted to the stairway. There she saw Kate and Lillian, fully clothed, coming down the stairs.

"What the hell are you doing, Lillian?" Mom asked. "Where are you taking her? And why is she dressed?" Mom's blood was starting to boil.

Lillian looked back at her sister as she helped Kate down. She offered her explanation in a serious and determined tone. "Norah," Lillian said, still moving, "she wants to go to school. Now *you* try to convince her that she can't!"

Norah looked at the two of them, thought about the craziness of the situation, then was overwhelmed by the sadness of it. She walked over to Kate on the landing, put her arms around her, and hugged her tight. "Oh, Ms. Hepburn," Mom said, fighting back tears, "you go back to bed now. It's late. Come. I'll take you." She shooed her sister downstairs and gently brought Kate back up. As they reached the top of the stairs, Kate turned, and in the demanding tone of days gone by, she commanded, "Norah, fire her!"

Mom's face broke into a slight smile. "Yes, Ms. Hepburn," she whispered as she helped Kate into bed, "I'll do that right now."

For Eileen
all good thanks Etc.
Katharine Hepburn

Letting Go

*D*uring Kate's last six months, between January and June of 2003, Mom would go back and forth between New York and Connecticut quite frequently. Kate's health had disintegrated to the point where she sometimes didn't know where she was. It was difficult to see her that way, but Norah had unfortunately gotten somewhat used to it.

Considering the situation, Fenwick was the perfect place for Kate to be. Everyone respected Kate's love of the water and made arrangements for her to continue enjoying the views. Kate slept upstairs, and the family installed a motorized chair to bring her up and down. In the living room, she could sit and look at the lapping water of the Long Island Sound for hours. Hospice care had been installed, and Kate was on oxygen. Because of this, her beloved fires could no longer be lit.

One day, after receiving a call from an executor of Kate's estate, Erik Hansen, who warned that Kate's condition had substantially worsened, Mom immediately went up to Fenwick. When she arrived, she found three of Dick's children, Ely, Thor, and Mundy, as well as Cynthia McFadden, already at the house. Over the course of the next few days, Norah let the cook leave and took over the preparation of everyone's meals. There was great comfort in doing what she did best—and what Kate would have wanted her to do. One by one, Hepburn family members continued to arrive—Kate's' younger brother, Dr. Bob; Peg; Katharine Houghton—and Norah took turns greeting each of them.

The day before Kate died, Liz Smith and Cynthia McFadden were there. While the ladies visited, Norah took Cynthia's son, Spencer, to the park. Mom was exhausted, both physically and mentally, but she wouldn't have wanted to be anywhere else.

The next morning, Mom was getting the day's meals ready. She was putting the final touches on her meat loaf, when the nurse walked in. Her look said it all. Everyone in the house who wasn't already upstairs went at once. Thor was reading to Kate from a book called *In Old New York*, but his aunt's eyes were closed. Mesmerized by the mellifluous sound of Thor's voice without hearing the exact words, all in the room were keenly aware that Kate was slipping away. Suddenly she was gone. Everybody stood together quietly for a while, then, one by one, they left the room.

Mom went down to the kitchen and mechanically began to set up the lunch she had prepared. She tried hard to focus on the task at hand. It wasn't as if she hadn't dealt with death before, and Kate's certainly had been anticipated. Still, the reality was numbing. She went through the motions of getting all the plates on the table. She thought about how blessed Kate was to have been surrounded by her loved ones—so many of them were there in the final days.

She served meat loaf, soup, and salad, followed by cookies and brownies.

While everyone ate, Norah slipped upstairs to pay her final respects. The door to Kate's was slightly ajar, and Norah gently pushed it open. Mom walked over and sat on the bed. She reached out and grasped her friend's hand. Her eyes filled with tears that overflowed onto her cheeks. Knowing that Kate wouldn't have approved of such sadness, she quickly wiped them away with a napkin she had in her apron.

Mom moved nearer and hugged Kate close. As she held her, she tenderly made the sign of the cross on the back of Kate's neck and whispered the prayer her father, Birdy, had taught her so many years ago: "The cross of Jesus, between us and harm, this day and forever, amen." She slowly released Kate's body and adjusted her on the soft white pillows. She pulled up the fluffy down comforter and glanced at Kate's thin, beautiful face. Thirty years of memories flashed through Norah's mind; she smiled and patted Kate's hand.

With a sigh of sadness mixed with joy, Mom stood up to go. Before leaving she turned to pronounce her last words to her friend: "How blessed I was to know and love you. Good-bye, Kate. And thank you."

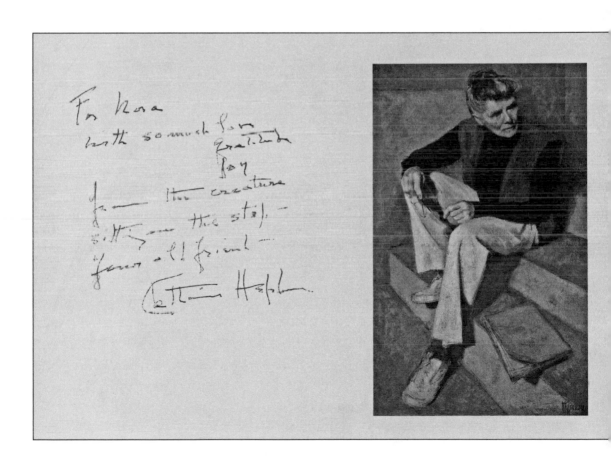

INDEX

Page numbers in italics indicate photographs.